PENGUIN HANDB

BUYING A HOUSE (

Lesley Vickers has spent several years learning her
way about the Law Courts and is an authority on
how to go from Fleet Street to Carey Street without
getting wet. She is a solicitor in London and an
experienced broadcaster on legal subjects.

L. E. Vickers

Buying a House or Flat

Fourth Edition

PENGUIN BOOKS

PENGUIN BOOKS

Published by the Penguin Group
27 Wrights Lane, London W8 5TZ, England
Viking Penguin Inc., 40 West 23rd Street, New York, New York 10010, USA
Penguin Books Australia Ltd, Ringwood, Victoria, Australia
Penguin Books Canada Ltd, 2801 John Street, Markham, Ontario, Canada L3R 1B4
Penguin Books (NZ) Ltd, 182–190 Wairau Road, Auckland 10, New Zealand

Penguin Books Ltd, Registered Offices: Harmondsworth, Middlesex, England

First published as *Buying a House* 1970
Revised and reissued under the present title 1977
Second edition 1981
Third edition 1985
Fourth edition 1990
1 3 5 7 9 10 8 6 4 2

Filmset in Monophoto Photina
Made and printed in Great Britain by
Richard Clay Ltd, Bungay, Suffolk

Warning

This book explains what experts are doing: it is
not a do-it-yourself book. Neither the publishers
nor the author accept responsibility for loss arising, through whatever cause, from anything
written in this book.

The law and practice described are those of
England and Wales, and may be different in Scotland.

To Chris, Chris, Chrissy and Kirsten.
Likewise to Julie, Peter,
Alex, Laura, Michael and Helen
with thanks for keeping me on the move.

Contents

Acknowledgements

I am most grateful to the Chief Land Registrar for allowing me the use of facsimile copies of entries of the Land Register, and to the Town Clerks of Ealing and Camden for information about the working of the Land Charges Departments. My thanks also go to my husband and to many friends and colleagues who helped with the present edition.

Part 1

The Search

Chapter 1

Mainly for First-Time Buyers

House-buying is not the stolid business it once was. Building societies used to be practically the only lenders on mortgage – now they have to compete with banks and mortgage companies. New lenders bring new ideas with them, the most successful being the sale of mortgages backed by insurance. Another is almost instant mortgage offers.

Many estate agents now belong to lending institutions and provide convenient points of sale for house, insurance and mortgage. Soon they will also be offering legal services. Wonderful news for first-time buyers? Well, yes and no. By looking at this book you have shown that you realize there is a lot to know about this business of house-buying. Read on, and you should soon recognize the difference between a poor bargain and a good one.

It would do no harm to put some of your savings into a building society and perhaps also in a bank deposit account. There is a great deal of money available for house loans at present, because many savers regard building societies as safe homes for investment and because finance companies at present consider house loans to be good business. Both these perceptions may change at any time, and we may return to waiting lists for would-be house-buyers. In the past, faithful savers often received priority when they needed a mortgage.

The great thing about the present glut of money for mortgages is that the potential house-buyer becomes a valued customer. Buying is made easy. Walk into an estate agent's to get details of a few houses and you may easily come out having applied for a mortgage you cannot afford and for insurance you did not know you needed. Or you may go to your bank to find out about a mortgage and come out with a lot of advice about insurance. This is fine, as long as you know how to judge the advice you are given. So far as I am aware, it is nobody's job to say: 'You don't need this kind of insurance at all'; nor, since building societies have largely given up being paternal, is it likely that anybody will say: 'This is a bad mortgage for you', or even 'Don't overstretch yourself'.

This chapter will outline some of the points a shrewd buyer will watch out for; they will be dealt with in greater detail later in the book.

The house Just as in the old days it is important to buy a solid house. You will find that the lenders, particularly if you want a high mortgage, will be keen on quality too. They want to ensure that should anything go wrong they will be able to recover their money. You yourself need to know a good deal more. Chapter 3 talks about good houses for high percentage loans, Chapter 10 about surveyors.

The loan The care with which your financial situation is examined may well depend on whether you want to borrow the bulk of the purchase price or only a small part. £55,000 lent on a £60,000 house leaves the lender (and you) more exposed than the same amount on a £100,000 house. It is fairly easy to get a large loan on an expensive house, indeed some advertisements stress that they specialize in high loans. Some lenders are prepared to lend large sums of money for high fees and to leave it to buyers to finance the loan as best they may. All this is dealt with in Chapters 3 and 4.

The cost The real cost is probably more than the first-time buyer has allowed for. There is much detail in Chapter 5.

When you know, roughly, what kind of house you want and can afford, contact one or two potential lenders to get a rough idea of what is on offer. Some questions about the rate of interest, about fees and about insurance would do no harm.

Perhaps you can at the same time ask for a mortgage certificate showing how much you will be able to borrow on a suitable house. Such a certificate can save a lot of time once you have found a house and may put you ahead in the queue if several people are keen on that house.

Many estate agents are as willing to sell insurance or mortgage as houses. Insurance companies, for example Prudential, or finance companies, for example Hambros, now own or work closely with firms of estate agents. Lloyds Bank owns the Black Horse agencies. Solicitors run property centres. The idea is for house, mortgage, all kinds of insurance and possibly even conveyancing all to be available under one roof. This 'supermarket' principle can save a lot of time but, to avoid regrets, do go into the property supermarket with your eyes open. It is one thing for a busy young couple to tolerate a wilting lettuce at the supermarket because they do not want to start queuing again at the greengrocers. Buying a speculative endowment policy when their prime need is security is rather more serious.

Not even this book can promise absolute security, but here are some hints designed to avoid major disappointment:

Be particularly alert if you are attracted to a deal advertised in the papers. Some financial services are very much more expensive and risky than others;

Do not at this stage sign *any* documents. Do not pay out *any* money;

If you visit estate agents to look at houses, concentrate on houses. Accept any brochures offered on other subjects and have a look at them when you get home. Regard any pressure with a little scepticism;

When you are ready to look seriously for a mortgage, you will, I hope, have read the two chapters in this book designed to assess what type of mortgage is likely to suit you.

Many mortgages on offer consist of a combination of two things: the mortgage proper and an insurance policy to cover that mortgage. There is no law to help you choose the best mortgage, but there are new rules under the Financial Services Act 1988 which may help with the choice of insurance. Estate agents, building societies, banks, brokers – as well as property supermarkets – fall into two categories: the first sells the product of only one insurance company. If it is not made clear whose policy is offered, I suggest you look elsewhere for insurance. Members of the other group, recognizable by the sign 'Member of Fimbra' (Financial Intermediaries, Managers and Brokers Regulatory Association), are authorized to offer independent advice on a wide range of policies and should be able to pick the one most suitable for you. You will normally be asked to complete a detailed questionnaire about yourself before taking out any life or similar policy. But, allow for the possibility that a particularly attractive mortgage is linked to an insurance policy not suited to your needs, or that it attracts heavy fees. Hence the importance of looking separately at house, mortgage and insurance. Soon, conveyancing (see pp. 148–52) may be included in the supermarket package. The problem is that there will then be no one to look after *your* interests as opposed to those of the lender or insurance company. So, if you are in any doubt, get two or three proposals and show them to your solicitor (see Chapter 8).

The enormous rise in house prices of the past few years means that in some parts of the country a person on an average wage cannot afford an average house. There are two possible ways around this problem:

(1) Try to buy with somebody else, ideally a wage-earning partner. More than two people can put their savings and earning power together and share for a few years in the hope of selling at enough profit to give them all a deposit for separate ventures. Get legal advice and remember that your maximum mortgage will probably take into account only the two largest incomes;

(2) Work out whether by moving further away from your place of work you can get a cheaper house. If that looks possible, try to work out whether what you spend on fares will be less than what you save on mortgage payments. The two might be close: so allow for the fact that there is tax relief on the first £30,000 mortgage, and, perhaps more importantly, that fares are likely to go up by more than mortgage interest rates over the next few years.

Personal factors count too: ask yourself how you would cope if your earnings took a dive, interest rates rose steeply, or your house dropped in value. It is not necessarily wise to jump at the biggest possible house or the biggest possible mortgage.

If past experience is anything of a guide to the future, money spent on a reasonable house is money well spent. So, spend it on good independent advice and on a sound building, rather than on the bathroom of your dreams and the prospect of a large but uncertain profit in the distant future.

Chapter 2

Where to Look for Your House

I had my first taste of house-hunting at the age of eleven, when my uncle, a writer, announced that he needed quiet surroundings for his work. My aunt and I spent the best part of that summer poring over Ordnance Survey maps and travelling along the country lanes of Scotland, Derbyshire, Devon and Wales. Country life, in however remote a spot, we found to include a great deal of barking, braying, crowing, hooting or whistling, none of which could be tolerated by my uncle. He eventually moved to a flat in Manchester, where noise was continuous and anonymous and where he wrote some of his most interesting books.

Like my uncle, Libby, who had recently been divorced, could choose to live anywhere in the country. Such a wide choice can be difficult. One of Libby's friends had carefully selected a district particularly awkward to reach from her ex-husband's home. She was defeated by the advent of a motor-way. Libby had been able to make a clean break when the marriage came to grief. She received a sum of money from the sale of the old house and intended using it for a new home for herself and the children, who were still below school age.

She drew up a rough list of her requirements:

Libby's first list
At least four rooms
Small town (she thought this would give her the best chance of finding reasonable schools for the children and part-time work for her-self).

Clearly, before Libby could seriously start house-hunting, she needed to be more precise and to decide on one or two areas in which to concentrate her search.

Should your choice be as wide as Libby's, start by deciding

roughly what kind of house you would like – town or country, old or new – and then buy a paper such as *Dalton's Weekly* or *Country Life* (depending on your purse and preference). You will get an idea of where you can find your kind of house at your kind of price. Bear in mind that house prices vary extraordinarily, often for reasons unconnected with the building: they are higher near town centres, in south-east England, in areas of full employment, in country areas easily reached from a big city.

For most house-buyers the initial search is more precise. They know roughly where they want to live: near their job, relatives, children's school, or whatever else may be particularly important to them. Their main problem is: can they get the kind of home they want for the kind of money they can afford.

Take, for example, Tom and May Jones, recently married. They have put their savings into two building societies. Tom is in his first job and intends to move on after about two years. May, as a teacher, is fairly mobile. One society is prepared to lend three times May's income plus Tom's for the past year; the other refuses to treat a wife's income as the major one and offers only three times Tom's annual income, as the main breadwinner, plus half of May's. The difference is sizeable. Tom next visits a couple of banks who are unenthusiastic when he mentions he wants a repayment mortgage. May gets an offer from a mortgage company – within a short time they have four mortgage proposals to compare (Chapters 3 and 4 talk of nothing but mortgages and will allow you to make your own comparisons).

Tom and May need a home which is easy to run, easy to sell when the time comes, and for which they will not need a large deposit. They want to spend as little time as possible on travelling to and from work, so they take out a map and start writing.

Tom and May's first list
Area – radius of five miles from work
Price – up to £x thousand
Accommodation – built since 1970, minimum three
rooms.

Peter is hoping for promotion. He would like to try for a job in London and expects to sell his very pleasant house in the Midlands at a good profit. His wife works part-time; they have three children. His settled income and the capital he will be able to put into a new house will make him welcome at bank, building society or mortgage company. The problem will be to find a home in or near London – where prices are high – as comfortable as his present one.

> *Peter's first list*
> Area – London
> Price up to £x thousand
> Accommodation – minimum eight rooms.

Your First List

It is as well not to go into too much detail with this first list, but rather to start finding out what kind of house can be had at what price in the chosen area. Four or five main points are quite enough.

How do you go about finding out? House-hunting is best done in two parts; part one can be usefully carried out from the depth of your armchair, with an occasional stroll to your newsagent or to the public library. The library can help you find the names of newspapers and freesheets in your chosen area. These papers will contain the names of local estate agents. Or, if you are lucky, there may be near you one of the property centres or a branch of a chain of estate agents who operate all over the country. It is worth spending a good deal of time and some money on this part of the hunt, particularly if you are moving to an area which is new to you. A few pounds spent on newspapers, maps and books about the area may stop you from buying the wrong house. Once you have studied the map you will begin to get an idea of what houses are worth visiting. This will save money, time and temper on fruitless visits. Once you know the price at which houses in particular roads tend to be offered you will have a better idea of how much you ought to pay.

What if you are buying at a time of fiercely rising prices? Can you afford the time to do all this patient spadework?

Probably not, but unless you have very suddenly come into money you will have gathered experience long before. You don't have to start house-hunting at the age of eleven, but try not to be pushed by inexperience and disappointment into buying the first house that is not snapped up under your nose. It may be available because it was turned down for a mortgage, or it may be overpriced.

What newspapers are most worth looking at? Most of the national newspapers carry house advertisements; some devote special days to houses. The Sunday papers also give a certain amount of information: you may well find that the Sunday papers you enjoy reading also carry advertisements for your kind of house.

Most newsagents stock one or several of the papers specializing in house advertisements. The most important and comprehensive are *Dalton's Weekly*, *Exchange and Mart* and, for London and the Home Counties, the *London Weekly Advertiser*. *What Mortgage* contains much useful information.

There are also the glossy monthly magazines. They deal chiefly with new estates in the course of being built and can be very useful if you are planning ahead: you will probably know the price well in advance, though you will have to check whether the builders reserve the right to put up prices. If you choose well, you ought to end up with a house designed for easy selling and possibly with a ready source of mortgage money. Estate developers frequently arrange with a particular source that it will grant mortgages to buyers of sufficiently high income. In times when there are more houses than buyers you sometimes get useful extras thrown in, for example a year's free mortgage or a fitted carpet.

Once the area of search has been roughly fixed, the local paper of that area is likely to prove the most useful guide to houses. The next step, therefore, is to find out what newspapers circulate in particular parts of the country. The newspapers will have a great many advertisements of houses for sale. Some of these are put in by the owners themselves, others by credit brokers, solicitors, or firms with vague titles like 'Financial Services'. From these descriptions you may get some idea of where the real expertise of the firm lies. But look also at other information, often tucked into a corner of such advertisements. It may tell you that the firm is the agent for a particular building society (and will therefore probably help you to get a mortgage from that source) or offer help in general terms with mortgage and insurance, which indicates that finance is their particular interest rather than the sale of houses. At this stage *you* want to know mainly about houses.

You are looking for two things in the advertisements: what kind of house can you get in that area for the money at your disposal? And who are the serious estate agents in the district? When you have looked at a few advertisements, and at details produced by one of the big chains, you can write to some of these agents and ask them for details of possible houses. When writing to an agent be careful not to do more than ask for particulars. You do not want unwittingly to engage an agent to find a house for you and to make yourself responsible for his fee.

A letter on the following lines is quite safe:

To a private advertiser

Dear Sir,

    I have seen your advertisement of a three-bedroomed house at the price of £   in today's *New Standard*. Could you please let me have particulars.

Yours faithfully,

To an estate agent

Dear Sir,

    I am looking for a three-bedroomed house in the Wythenshawe area, if possible built between 1930 and 1939. Price up to £

    Could you please let me have particulars of houses which might be suitable. Is the one in   Road advertised in today's *New Standard* still available?

Yours faithfully,

You can, without incurring any liability for estate agents' fees, write similar letters to as many agents as you wish. The result will probably be a flood of printed matter. Most of this you will find useful chiefly as scribbling paper, but gradually you will get an idea of the kind of house you can expect for the price which you are prepared to pay.

If this is a time when prices are shooting up faster than the daffodils (wild price rises usually happen in spring) and you must join the rush, here are a few hints:

if possible don't buy before you have explored the market;

in times of shortage, keep in close touch with the more active estate agents in your chosen area. They may well not send circulars when houses are snapped up on their doorstep;

when houses are easy to sell, many owners sell privately. Tell your friends and colleagues at work that you are looking for a house. They may know someone who wants to sell;

you could even try pushing circular letters through a few letter boxes in your favoured district, but make it clear you are not an estate agent in disguise. You could try something like:

My wife and I are desperate for a house in or near   as I am starting a new job on   . Do you happen to know anyone who wants to sell? We should be so grateful if you would let us know and shall of course refund your expenses. We have been promised a mortgage in principle and could pay up to £

Don't forget your address and telephone number at home and at work. It is a long shot, but it could work.

Before you decide how much you can afford to pay for a new home, please read the chapters on mortgages and on what it costs to buy and run a home. There was a time when banks and building societies were cautious lenders who often irritated house-buyers by deciding on maximum loans well below the buyer's needs. At present (late 1989) many lenders are quite happy to hand out large amounts on mortgage. Unfortunately, an increasing number of house-buyers, particularly if they have large endowment policies, find after a time that they cannot afford the monthly mortgage payments, and as a result some of them lose their homes. But with proper planning you can almost certainly avoid disaster. Do not get carried away; do your figures, and then decide what you can afford. After this you will probably want to make a second list, a sadder and wiser list, distinguishing between essentials and desirables.

Tom and May talked to their local estate agent and looked at various newspapers. They came to the conclusion that their choice was between a rented flat, a new house outside the town or a Victorian house which they could work on and which they might be able to sell at a better price.

Tom and May's second list
Area – not more than 5 miles from work
Price – £x, but preferably £5,000–£7,000 less
Accommodation – three-room flat or three-room conversion.

Libby had by now decided to look for a terrace house on an estate with lots of young families. She rang some of the well-known developers and received details of houses built during the past few years. She eventually decided to concentrate on an area about twenty miles distant from her mother. She deferred a decision on whether to put most of her money into a new house – either buying a bigger one or moving to a more expensive area – or whether to buy a more modest house and put money away for emergencies. Once upon a time saving was a great virtue. At a time of high inflation and low rates of interest, saving in a bank or building society account may be an assured way of losing money. Many people spend as much as they dare on buying their house.

Libby's second list
Area – Waverley Road or Glentree Estate
Town house
Price – up to £x thousand
Walking distance first school, playgroup, park.

Peter realized that he had to choose between the comforts of a house well away from London and a humbler living standard in the capital. Although salaries may be higher in London, his extra earnings would not pay for a considerably higher mort-gage. He decided on comfort and employment in the country. He applied for jobs and after each hopeful interview bought the local newspapers. The second list was easily made as soon as Peter had a definite job offer.

Peter's second list
Area – within 10 miles of place of work
Near school – or within easy reach
Large garden

Price – approximately four times* Peter's earnings – perhaps slightly more if he got a good price for his present house.

One house was rejected because it was a long way from the village. Peter's wife did not really want to drive a car, and did not trust herself to remember every bit of shopping if she could reach a shop only once a week.

Another house was advertised as being close to the water's edge, overlooking the river. Peter knew that the river was tidal and the chances were that for some six hours each day the house would overlook not water, but mud. An inquiry of the agent confirmed this: although neither estate agent nor owner is under any duty to volunteer information about the demerits of a house, they must give honest answers to questions. If they mislead you, you may have a legal claim against them. In any event, a muddy river-bed – a smelly source of danger to a frustrated sailor – may be a source of delight to an observer of wildlife.

At the same time as looking for a house, Peter and his wife also looked for suitable schools for their children and decided to try to find a house within walking distance of a primary school for their two younger children. When the children were old enough to go to a secondary school they would be able to cope with a bus journey.

Your Second List

After a few weeks of looking at newspapers, answering advertisements and corresponding with estate agents, you will have enough information to make a visit worth while, even if it means travelling some distance. Prepare for the visit by:

* This is not a fixed formula. You can easily:
   (i) work out approximately how much you will get for your present house;
   (ii) deduct your present mortgage and the expenses connected with the sale and the move;
   (iii) add your new mortgage, then make your decision.
   Peter, in London, would probably need the maximum mortgage he could get on his income. In a less popular part of the country, he could manage on a good deal less.

reading at least Part I of this book, and also reading about the particular type of home which interests you, e.g. flats, new houses, leaseholds. You can easily find the relevant bits from the index at the end of the book;

arming yourself with a map or street guide. You may well be able to borrow this from your public library;

telling some of the estate agents that you will be coming, and asking whether they can arrange for you to see houses;

fixing appointments with a few house-owners.

The agent who looks most like having your kind of home may be willing to take you to several houses: a great convenience if you travel by public transport. But leave enough time for going round the district on your own – wander round and get the feel of the neighbourhood. What shops are there? You do not merely want to know where the nearest supermarket is, but whether the shops and the shoppers are homely or smart or exotic. How well do they look after their houses? If they neglect them, it will do your own house no good. Is there a bookshop, betting shop, theatre, tennis club, church, Rotary Club, bingo hall, disco, park, playground – or whatever your family is interested in? Where are the schools (if you have children), doctor or hospital (if you have invalids in the family)? Are there any motorways, factories or flightpaths?

You may already know the answers if the area is one with which you are familiar. If you are moving to a new area try to find time for just roaming. Walk around pubs, shopping centres and cafés; look for clubs and discotheques. This not only makes for a pleasant afternoon but may stop you from moving to a place where you would feel uncomfortable.

The more time you can spend on this part of your search the better. You are more likely to find out whether you would settle happily and how much you should expect to pay for the kind of house you would like.

Some Hints for Different Types of Buyer

Moderate Savings, Moderate Income

The choice will probably be between a new house, a converted flat or a small purpose-built flat.

New flats are becoming smaller all the time; if well built and well planned, however, they make a good first purchase. Some builders throw in a number of goodies with which to tempt you, for example, legal fees, carpets, a TV set. Allow for the fact that these are unlikely to be 'free' and check that the flat itself is worth what you are paying. If you buy carefully, you should make a profit when you sell, particularly in an area where there is a shortage of building land.

A new or newish house on an estate often makes a good family home and is easily resold. It will probably cost more than a flat, old or new, in the same area. Nevertheless, if you have the choice, a house may be better value than a flat. You pay less per square foot and the extra space can give you more scope.

Flats, converted out of Victorian or Edwardian family houses, are very popular with young buyers. You get a lot of space for your money, lending institutions are prepared to grant as high a mortgage for them as for newer flats, and you can use your energy and ingenuity in making the most of your purchase. But allow for repairs – all old houses need them almost constantly – and also allow for the higher cost of decorating and heating. Your solicitor will be able to tell whether you are responsible under the lease for keeping your own flat in good repair, or for a share of the cost of repairing the entire building. If the latter, do get a surveyor's report on the whole house before you commit yourself to buying: a new roof can cost a lot of money.

A small family will probably find a small modern house the best buy. Such a property tends to keep its price and be easily saleable, and the mortgage payments should not be crippling. A larger family is more comfortable in a bigger house. It may also, with luck, have enough able-bodied members to help pay the mortgage and assist with the repairs an older building inevitably needs and keeps needing.

Low Savings, Rising Income

Take maximum mortgage. Consider borrowing on second mortgage to buy the best house within your grasp. Make sure the lenders allow you to pay off the second and part of the first mortgage from time to time without having to pay a penalty. Your rising income should enable you to reduce the mortgage as time goes on. But watch out. Your low savings may be due to your expensive tastes.

Two or More People Sharing

There is tax relief for the resident owner of a house or flat on the first £30,000 of a mortgage. There is no additional tax relief if ownership is shared, whether the owners are married or not. People will buy together either because they enjoy one another's company, or because they do not have enough money to buy separate homes. A two-roomed flat tends to be a lot cheaper than two studio flats; a larger house may lend itself to conversion into separate units, but this is a long-term project needing both money and persistent effort.

You should be able to get a mortgage based on the two biggest of several incomes. But do assess the personal as well as the financial implications of a joint purchase and make sure that each contributor's interest is recorded in the deeds of ownership. (See Chapter 8).

Previous Mortgage Problems

If you were refused a mortgage in the past when two and a half times the main income was about the most you could borrow, you may find it possible now to get a better mortgage offer. A lot more money is available for lending.

Even if you have a bad record – have outstanding judgments against you or have lost a previous home because you did not pay your mortgage – all is not necessarily lost. Study the newspapers for offers of non-status mortgages. Such mortgages are offered without much enquiry into your past, but be warned: they are usually a good deal more costly than the standard mortgage.

Older People

Older people should usually aim at paying off the mortgage before retirement. Try to take up your last big mortgage by the age of about fifty (if not before). In an assured occupation you can get a fifteen-year mortgage without much difficulty. A person with a good pension could well consider leaving a small mortgage outstanding because of its welcome tax relief: it may make it possible to buy a slightly more luxurious house.

When there is a good supply of mortgage money available, older people may be able to take out a new mortgage under which they pay interest during their lifetime and the capital is repaid on their death, rather than at the end of a fixed period.

Many people move house when they retire. Consider before you cut yourself off from friends and relatives whether the seaside or the isolated cottage is the best place for you in the unfriendly days of February. If you plan to retire a long way from your present home, try to get to know the place of your choice and its people before breaking all your links with home. Maybe you work in town and already have a cottage in the country to which you want to retire. You can sell your 'main residence' in town free of capital gains tax and move to the country.

Sheltered Housing for the Elderly

Small bungalows and flats are now being specially built for the elderly. There is usually provision for a resident warden who can be called in an emergency. The layout of each bungalow or flat should make it easy for elderly people to move around. Well planned accommodation should provide for easy access to the door, for moving about in a wheelchair if necessary, for electric plugs to be at table height, and for an alarm system allowing people to contact the warden.

Before you buy, there are a lot of important questions to be asked. Can you sell your home as you wish, or are there restrictions? A home which has to be offered to the original seller at the original price may not produce enough money for you to move somewhere else. Is there enough health-care available to allow you to stay in the place if you become less able to look after yourself? Are there restrictions on who can live in the place? There are schemes for a kind of shared ownership between developer and elderly buyer: instead of buying the home you merely buy the right to live there for as long as you wish. Check how much you would get should you need to move after a few years. And if you have children, check whether they would be disappointed if you were not able to leave them a house under your will.

The buying and selling of sheltered accommodation is not always as simple as with ordinary flats and houses, and it is most important for anyone interested in buying to get independent legal advice.

Advantages: You own your home

Your home is saleable

The warden can help if you are disabled or become ill

Snags: 24-hour warden service is expensive

The more comprehensive the service, the more it will cost

Check carefully: Does the service charge include hot water, central heating, upkeep of the garden, maintenance of the outside of the building, repainting the inside?

How many wardens are there? One warden cannot be on duty 24 hours a day, 7 days a week.

Is there an easy-to-use alarm system in every room, including kitchen and W C?

How far from shops, buses, doctor, hospital etc. is the house?

Is there double glazing, roof insulation? If the house is draughty, heating costs will be higher.

Moving in a Hurry

If you are faced with a sudden move and no time to explore, it is probably wisest to choose a newish standard house, for example in a terrace built during the last fifteen years, or a semi-detached house up to forty years old. It is relatively easy to find out the current price for such properties and to sell them again when you have found one nearer your ideal. Also, you should get a mortgage without too much trouble. Buying from an owner who has already found a house to move to may be quicker than buying from someone who has only recently decided to move and who may change his or her mind or fail to get a mortgage.

Important: For All Would-Be House-Buyers

It is cheaper to borrow on mortgage than to take out a bank overdraft or to juggle your credit cards. Also, there is tax relief on a mortgage up to a limit of £30,000. Therefore if you need to buy both a house and a car, it is cheaper to pay cash for the car and to take out a bigger mortgage on the house than to borrow on both.

Chapter 3

A Thicket of Mortgages

Everyone knows that you can buy a house or a flat without having the money to pay for it. The beauty is that large sums can be borrowed much more cheaply for buying houses and flats than for anything else you might buy on credit. You may be used to the idea of borrowing money to buy things, but there is a difference: a car or a washing machine loses its value quickly – therefore the repayments, at a high rate of interest, must be made fairly quickly. A house is expected to go up in value – therefore you can borrow over a longer period and at a lower interest rate.

Of course, it is not all jam. No lender will lend without a mortgage: a burden which will be with you for many years to come. 'Mort-gage' literally means 'dead pledge'. So before you commit yourself to any offer, whether temptingly advertised or not, please read on. This chapter will try to make your dead pledge as light as possible.

First, about mortgages in general. Wherever the money comes from, house loans have much in common:

(1) You will get a loan only if the lender approves of your house, yourself and your income.

(2) You have to pay interest on the mortgage and will probably get tax relief.

(3)You will have to sign (and obey the terms of) a mortgage document.

(4) You will not get the deeds of the house while you owe any money under the mortgage.

(5) The type of mortgage most warmly recommended is not necessarily the one that is best for you.

The House

Lenders (also known as mortgagees) like best to put money into a house built traditionally of bricks or stone and with a tiled roof, either detached, semi-detached or terraced. A modern purpose-built leasehold flat will be equally popular. A house should be either freehold or on a very long lease. 'Freehold' means that both the house and the ground on which it stands belong to their owner for ever. 'Leasehold' means that the ground underneath the house belongs to *A* who lets the house itself on a long lease (often 99 or 999 years) to *B*. At the end of the lease the ownership of the house goes back to *A*, or – more likely – to his great-grandson, or to the person who has in the meantime bought the freehold reversion from *A*. If there are only a few years of a lease left, no building society is likely to lend *B* money on it. First-time buyers should therefore keep clear of the end of a long lease till they have taken advice from a solicitor. The house could be a bargain if the Leasehold Reform Act allows the occupier to buy the freehold (more about this in Chapter 8). If it does not, or if the freehold costs too much, don't buy that house. Anyone with small savings and the need for the largest possible mortgage loan should look for a newish house, flat or maisonette.

If you have set your heart on an older house or flat, you may be able to get a high mortgage, but you will also have to allow for the higher costs of repairing and maintaining your home. Frequently a building society says that certain repairs must be done before it will hand over the loan money. In recent years many old family houses have been divided into separate flats. A long lease (usually at least 99 years) is then granted for each separate 'converted' flat and each flat can be sold and resold independent of the other flats in the house. Often, instead of making the owner of the top floor flat responsible for the entire roof, the cost of all major repairs is shared by all the flats in the building. Converted flats are popular with young couples – they are larger and may cost less than modern homes.

Mortgages can usually also be had for purpose-built flats and for maisonettes. A 'flat' usually shares its door to the street and its stairs with other flats; a 'maisonette' does not.

The House-Buyer

Most building societies are far more interested in the purchasers' income than in the purchasers themselves. Their age matters to some extent: you must be at least eighteen years old before you are allowed to own a house, while at the other end, lenders prefer mortgages to be repaid before retirement. People in their fifties may therefore have greater difficulty in borrowing money on mortgage than people in their twenties, and will have to accept a mortgage for a shorter term. However, if you have had a mortgage for many years and have always punctually paid your monthly instalments, you will probably have no difficulty in getting another mortgage from the same society, whatever your age. Equally, if you can look forward to an assured pension, the building society will probably welcome you as a borrower.

The applicant's sex matters less than it used to: a woman with an assured income will have very little difficulty in borrowing. Complaints often come from women in freelance occupations who resent being patronized by building society managers. However, their male counterparts find it equally hard to get a loan before their business is visibly well established. Traditional lenders are keen on seeing audited accounts for at least two consecutive years, showing a healthy profit.

Your Income

This is of far greater interest to the lenders than personal circumstances, but here again different lenders use different yardsticks. Some look at gross income – the amount you earn on paper, disregarding tax, etc. – others at net income – the amount you actually take home each week or month; a few don't look at all. Some want to know about your lifestyle so far, others take no interest in your spending habits. Some lenders take overtime into account, some consider all the earnings of both husband and wife, others only a small part of the second income. Some are willing to take into account the income you will get from letting part of the house, others will refuse to lend on a house which is not entirely occupied by you and your family. Having decided on what they consider to be your 'income', different lending organizations use varying formulae for calculating the maximum amount they are prepared to lend. Most lenders look at the 'main' income first. This, where several people are buying a house together, could be the biggest or it might be the steadiest income. Some lenders look on female borrowers as potential childbearers rather than as main income providers. A mortgage offer will probably be in the region of three times the main annual income plus one or one and a half times a second income; some lenders go still higher. People with high incomes are positively encouraged by some firms to take out high loans, often without too much checking of their incomes. Against this, lenders will not usually take into account more than two incomes, regardless of how many people club together to buy. Nor are they usually concerned with whether the buyers are or are not related.

The big difference these days is that instead of weeping at the door of the building society, begging them to lend you enough to put a roof over your head, you are now a valued customer of big business. Large and important companies fall over themselves with eagerness to grant mortgages on more attractive terms than the competition. Advertisements appear in newspapers and on TV tempting you with wonderful bargains. So it is worth becoming streetwise. The rest of this chapter will explain what the lenders are talking about and will make it easier for you to ask questions about things they have not told you but which are important to you. The next chapter will talk of some of the insurance-linked mortgages on offer.

There is a great variety of mortgages and new ones are constantly introduced by banks, building societies, insurance companies and finance companies. Some of these 'new' qualities are more real, some more important, than others.

Building Society Mortgage

The basic traditional building society mortgage is for a fixed amount at a variable rate of interest payable over a fixed period.

Fixed amount means that the amount you borrow is clearly stated in the mortgage document. That fixed amount can nevertheless, by agreement, be varied. For instance, when interests go up, you may be keen for the extra to be added to your mortgage debt rather than to your monthly payments. Also, check whether you can repay chunks of capital from time to time (you may get a large bonus or legacy) and on what terms.

Variable means that interest rates go up or down following variations in the Bank of England base rate; changes in interest charged by building societies tend to be much the same whichever society you borrow from. They depend mainly on the interest rates a society has to pay its depositors – you will have to pay slightly more to the building society than the society pays them. Usually, borrowers' monthly payments do not change until a good number of weeks after a change in the base rate. Even then, borrowers are sometimes asked if they would prefer to pay at the old rate and have the excess added to the mortgage debt.

Building societies tend to calculate the balance you owe on mortgage once every year and to charge interest on that balance. If you have a repayment mortgage and therefore repay a little of the capital each month, then towards the end of that year you are probably paying at a slightly higher rate of interest – hence the duty of any lender to tell you the APR (annual percentage rate), the rate of interest you really pay.

Fixed period The loan may be for 25 years. But when you sell the house during the 25 years you will be expected to repay the mortgage. Also, when interest rates go up, you may be able to extend the mortgage term rather than pay more interest each month.

Bank Mortgage and Finance Company Mortgage

A typical bank or finance company mortgage is essentially similar to a building society one. But there are a few differences.

Not all such mortgages state clearly the amount you are borrowing. The mortgage deed may well talk of 'all moneys payable for the time being by the borrower to the lender'. This harmless phrase means that if the bank lends you more money, for whatever purpose, after you have taken out the mortgage, that loan may also be secured by your house.

Some banks and mortgage institutions offer LIBOR-linked mortgages. LIBOR (London Interbank offered rate) changes less erratically than the base rate. LIBOR rates are usually fixed at three-monthly intervals, but are of course also influenced by what goes on in the world outside and the rate at which the lenders themselves can borrow in the money market. The importance to borrowers is that changes in LIBOR are quickly followed by changes in the monthly payments required from them. Building society changes tend to take longer; quick changes benefit a borrower when interest payments drop, slow changes when they go up.

Banks tend to calculate outstanding debts daily or weekly; if their lending rate is also lower than that of a building society mortgage, it may be cheaper to borrow from the bank. But check whether there is an initial fee to pay.

Another possible difference is that some banks fix the monthly mortgage payments a year ahead whatever the lending rate, so you can therefore budget for that year. The adjustment is made for the following year. Some lenders, instead of asking you to increase your monthly payments, add any shortfall to the outstanding capital – useful when interest rates are up and your house has increased in value.

However, the main difference is not between banks and mortgage companies on the one hand and building societies on the other; as you have seen, many of their qualities overlap. The big decision you will have to make is whether to take out a *repayment* or an *endowment* mortgage.

Repayment or Endowment Mortgage?

Are you going to choose a repayment mortgage and gradually pay back the money you have borrowed by small monthly instalments over the years? Or will you leave the whole loan outstanding until you sell or the lenders ask for their money back? If you are not repaying the capital as you go along, the lenders will require you to take out an insurance policy which is mortgaged to them in the same way as your house. You will have to pay monthly interest on the house loan and also a monthly premium on an insurance policy which, ideally, guarantees the full amount of the loan. Whether it lives up to this aim is something about which you will have to ask searching questions before you commit yourself. Policies range from those which assuredly cover the amount of the mortgage and offer the chance of a handsome bonus on top to those which guarantee nothing. There is more about insurance policies in the next chapter.

One of the arguments against repayment mortgages is that in the later years there is less tax relief because by then you will owe less money to the lender. Let us look at tax relief.

MIRAS – Mortgage Interest Relief at Source

If up to now you have been paying rent, you might be in for a pleasant surprise. Buying a house as your principal (or your only) home entitles you to tax relief on up to £30,000 of your mortgage at your highest rate of income tax. Tax at the basic rate is automatically deducted. If your mortgage document says that your interest rate is 10 per cent, you in fact pay only 7.5 per cent. This is one of the few occasions in life when a loan is cheaper than the complicated documents make out. Better still, people who do not have to pay tax still get the tax relief. This helps anyone who becomes unemployed or whose income has dropped.

Tax at the higher rate is not always deducted at source. If it is not, tell your Inspector of Taxes and ask for a higher PAYE code number.

A word of warning: a monthly mortgage payment can be calculated in different ways. If you have a traditional repayment mortgage (known as a rising net repayment mortgage) then at the beginning of the mortgage term you are paying mainly interest and you will get more tax relief in the early years than in the later years. Since the introduction of MIRAS, many building societies have used a different system (the annuity or constant net repayment mortgage) under which you pay the same net amount each month. The first system benefits you if you are planning to move again fairly soon; the new system is slightly cheaper in the long run. Bear in mind that repayment mortgages generally get better tax relief in the first ten years or so than during the last ten, because the bulk of the monthly payment during the first ten years is interest. The disadvantages, from a tax point of view, of repayment mortgages become important only if you live in the same house with the same mortgage for all its twenty or thirty years.

Bear in mind also that there is no tax relief on insurance premiums.

Mortgage Protection Policies and Endowment Policies

If you are going to opt for a repayment mortgage you would be unwise to go without insurance against your own death before the mortgage is paid off. Indeed many lenders insist on this. A mortgage protection policy of this kind is quite different from an endowment or a life policy. Mortgage protection insures against an event which may never happen at all (most people live to pay off their mortgages), whereas an endowment policy will mature and will have to be paid out at some time. It stands to reason that a mortgage protection premium is much lower than an endowment premium. In fact, however, a repayment mortgage is not necessarily cheaper than an endowment mortgage. The rates charged depend not only on the factors outlined earlier but also on the kind of mortgage any particular lender wants to sell at any particular time.

If you are considering an endowment mortgage of whatever type it is important to get quotations from several insurance companies. Mortgage brochures often leave out the monthly endowment premium (which you have to pay in addition to monthly mortgage interest) because it varies from person to person. Make sure you compare like with like by asking each company for a detailed quotation based on the same assumptions, e.g. a mortgage for twenty-five years for £x thousand at y per cent for a man aged thirty, secured by a with-profits endowment policy. You could ask for two different quotations, the second for a low start policy or for a policy on the joint lives of a husband and wife. The difference in price between 'single life' and 'joint lives' of husband and wife is often quite small. A joint lives policy means that the policy money is paid out on the death of either the husband or the wife before the end of the mortgage term.

When you have found out which companies offer a good bargain, check how easy it would be to transfer the policy to another house should you want to move during its currency – as you almost certainly will. Taking an endowment mortgage does not mean that you are stuck with the same house for the next twenty-five years. When you sell your house, you have three options:

(1) You can keep your policy going. If you are taking out a bigger mortgage on the new house, you can take out a further insurance policy for the excess. Or you can divide your mortgage: endowment for the original amount, repayment for the balance.

(2) You can make your insurance policy a 'paid up policy'. This means that you pay no further premiums but leave your past payments with the insurance company till the policy matures. You will obviously get less at the end of the twenty-five years than if you continue paying.

(3) You surrender the policy for a cash sum. Be sure to get comparative figures from the insurance company before you decide. Surrender values can be disappointingly low.

You are unlikely to find an ordinary endowment policy a particularly good bargain. But endowment mortgages do have advantages for some people:

Advantages: The policy can act as health insurance: it cannot be cancelled whatever your state of health might be in the future

Tax relief is greater than under repayment scheme as your debt is not paid off during the currency of the mortgage

Low life insurance premiums for young borrowers

Life insurance continues even if you sell the house

Snags: No tax relief on premium payments

Insurance premiums continue even if you sell the house

Surrender value of policy may be small

If mortgage interest rate goes up, your monthly payments will have to go up – the mortgage term is not easily extended

The profits element in a 'with-profits' policy is based on hope; there is no guarantee of profits

Some insurances turn out much better than others.

Perhaps you feel that the time for buying has not yet come, the venture is too expensive. Do not despair. Go on saving for a while and see whether you can take advantage of a Home Loan.

Home Loan

This loan is unlikely to solve your mortgage problem but is a pleasant extra offered by the state to first-time buyers. This is what you have to do to qualify:

(1) Open a home loan account with a building society or savings bank. You have to fill in a special form: make sure to ask for this – you cannot join the scheme until you have filled in the right piece of paper.

(2) Save into that account for two years.

(3) Put at least £300 in the account by the end of Year One.

(4) Keep at least £300 in the account for the whole of Year Two.

(5) Better still, bring your account up to £600 before applying for a mortgage.

(6) £600, when you apply for the mortgage, qualifies you for an extra mortgage loan of £600, interest free for up to five years. £300 or more in the account for all of the year before you apply for a mortgage qualifies for a tax-free bonus of between £40 (for a £300 deposit) and £110 (for £1,000 or more).

(7) The best sum to keep in the account would seem to be £300 in the first year and £1,000 in the second. This will give tax-free interest of £110 plus an extra loan of £600 which can be added to your mortgage.

(8) The scheme can be used only for houses below price limits laid down by the government. The limits in 1986 ranged from £25,800 in Humberside to £63,100 in Greater London and are changed from time to time.

Chapter 4

The Best Mortgage?

As a general rule, the longer your mortgage term, the less you pay each month. True, your payments will go on longer too, but the pound you are saving today is bound to be worth more than the extra pound you may have to pay in twenty-five years.

Fixed or variable interest? The last chapter talked about how variable interest rates are worked out in different ways by different lenders. A mortgage at fixed interest is in a class of its own. It is the only one where you know precisely what the mortgage is going to cost each month. The one thing you cannot know at the start is whether this is going to compare well or ill with what other people will have to pay in the future. More about fixed interest mortgages on p. 46.

A repayment mortgage brings another kind of certainty: you know that all you have to do to get rid of your mortgage debt is to make the monthly mortgage payments you are asked for.

But let's face it: most of the brochures, the advertisements, the quotations rely on the prospect of your taking out some kind of insurance policy to pay back your loan. The rest of this chapter will describe some of the policies on offer; they may come under different names or may combine some of the schemes I have mentioned separately. Even if in the end you decide against all of them, you will want to know what is on offer in order to make an informed decision.

All mortgages in this chapter have one thing in common: your monthly interest payments are just that. They do not repay any of the money you borrowed. That money should come out of an insurance policy. Although we talk of different types of mortgage, it is the insurance policies rather than the mortgages which come in many varieties, not necessarily under the names used in the headings. Some insurance policies guarantee a minimum sum when they mature, others do not.

A new distinction was introduced by the Financial Services Act 1988. In the olden days brokers could make vague recommendations. Now, they must either be linked to a particular insurance company or provide independent advice. Quite what standards they are to use is not clear at the time of writing.

The building society or estate agency may well produce only one insurance quotation because it is 'tied' to one particular insurance company. It is important for you to get details of several policies from different sources. Find out whether you have to buy the whole package, or whether you can choose the mortgage and insurance that suit you best. Find out whether the insurance policy guarantees the mortgage in full. If not, to what extent does the final amount depend on the company making a consistent profit? Who are the insurance company, how profitable have they been over the past twenty years? It may be wise to cover a possible shortfall by a separate insurance policy. What follows are examples of policies which might be on offer. For the pros and cons of endowment policies in general, see p. 55.

With-Profits Endowment

You take out a policy for the full amount of the mortgage. The policy shares in the profits of the insurance company, declared every so often. At the end of the mortgage period you should therefore get a capital sum (representing your share of the profits) in addition to having your mortgage repaid. Lovely – but remember that this bonanza won't reach you for another twenty or twenty-five years, even if you sell your house and repay your mortgage in a few years from now. In twenty years an amount that now buys a house may well only buy a car.

Without-Profits Endowment

This is similar to the other endowment policy, except that the monthly insurance premium is lower and there is no bonanza at the end of the mortgage term. The mortgage is repaid when the policy matures, and that's it.

Not usually a good idea.

Low Cost Endowment

Instead of an insurance policy to protect the whole mortgage, the insurance company will offer an endowment policy with profits for, say, half of the loan, coupled with a 'term insurance' for the other half. That combined premium is lower than the premium for an ordinary endowment policy with profits, and the term insurance makes sure that the mortgage can be repaid should you die during the mortgage term. In a good scheme the policy will be worth more than the amount you will eventually need to repay your mortgage. Unfortunately some schemes are based on optimism rather than on sound financial planning. Some schemes have *no* guaranteed sum at the end of the mortgage period. The monthly payments may be lower than for a repayment mortgage, but you may not get enough at the end of the day to pay off your mortgage.

This is a popular arrangement, and can be excellent, but be sure to ask all the right questions.

Fixed Interest

A scheme much used abroad and gradually being introduced in this country. You take out a mortgage on which your interest is fixed, usually for the first three or five years. At the end of that period either your mortgage automatically becomes a variable interest one or you negotiate terms for a further mortgage. There is usually provision for switching to variable interest or for early redemption of the mortgage – often at additional expense to the borrower.

Interest rates are usually a little below variable rates at the time the mortgage is taken out. So, if you are borrowing at a time of low interest rates you may get an excellent bargain. The difficulty is to guess whether interest rates will go up or down.

You will probably find that the lenders insist on some kind of endowment policy.

A fixed interest mortgage may do wonders for your peace of mind, provided you can bear the thought that though you started at a lower rate of interest than others, their interest may just possibly come down below yours.

Not all lending institutions offer fixed interest mortgages.

Mortgage Plus Guarantee Policy

No lender wants to hand over more than 70 to 80 per cent of its valuation of a house out of its own funds. In fact, however, there are many loans of 90 per cent and 95 per cent. The top slice of the loan is guaranteed by an insurance policy for which you pay one single premium instead of the more usual annual premium. This once-only premium will probably be at least four per cent of the sum guaranteed. The lender will either deduct the premium from the mortgage amount or, if you are lucky, will lend it to you and recover it gradually and comparatively painlessly over the run of the mortgage.

Snag: You may not have allowed for the guarantee policy when making your plans; it does not tend to be very loudly advertised.

100 Per Cent Mortgage

Some of the newer lenders go further and offer 100 per cent of the value of the house, provided the loan falls within its income limits (typically 3–3½ times the borrower's income or 2¾–3¼ times joint income). The rate of interest charged tends to be higher than on an ordinary building society mortgage. The interest rate on a guarantee policy will also be higher, probably 7 per cent, and you need to make careful inquiries about the kind of endowment policy you are expected to buy. The lender will probably collect the premium from you at the start: a 7 per cent premium on a 25 per cent excess on a mortgage of £50,000 would cost about

£875. Some lenders charge high fees for arranging such a mortgage. You might prefer to go on saving for a while.

Advantage: You may be able to buy a home although your savings are small.
Snag: Not cheap.

Tenants of local authorities with the right to buy their homes at a discount are in a special position – see Chapter 12.

Top-up Loan

Not a mortgage to choose, but one you may have to put up with if you cannot borrow as much money as you need. It is possible that an insurance company will agree to lend the balance on a second mortgage at a higher rate of interest and subject to an endowment policy, probably on the whole amount of the two mortgages. Such a loan can be very expensive at the time it is made but is popular in times of high inflation. The first years may be tough, but as payments are pegged while the value of your house and your income go up, this kind of arrangement has followers among rising young executives.

Advantages: High mortgage possible
May help you buy more expensive house
Snags: High cost of buying – legal fees for house and for two mortgages
High monthly payments – two mortgages plus insurance premium
Tax relief only up to £30,000 mortgage
High interest rate on second mortgage
Not every lender uses this scheme.

Non-Status Mortgage

Usually a lender wants to be reassured about a borrower's earnings so far. Where the borrower cannot satisfy a lender (perhaps because he has only just started in business, or because he has incurred heavy debts in the past) it is sometimes possible to get a loan on stringent terms rather like those for 100 per cent mortgages, and with similar pros and cons. You are unlikely to be able to borrow more than 65 per cent.

Low Start Mortgage

Instead of paying the same amount year after year, you pay less in the early years of the mortgage and more later. The maximum rate of payment is usually reached at the end of either five or ten years. Some insurance companies combine the low cost endowment scheme with a 'low start' scheme, where insurance premiums start low but go up every year. They may continue to rise throughout the currency of the policy.

Advantages: Costs less than other mortgages at the start

May bring a house within your reach when you are only beginning to earn

You may be able to get a higher loan than with other mortgage schemes

Higher mortgage payments in the future may be affordable because your income has gone up

Snags: The cost of the mortgage may go up faster than your income

Payments may be high when your children are at their most expensive and when you or your spouse is not earning

Interest on this sort of mortgage may be higher than usual.

Index Linking

Another way of starting with comparatively low monthly payments.

As with an ordinary repayment mortgage, your monthly payments consist of a combination of interest and capital. The rate of interest charged by the lender is lower than usual, and the loan can be as high as $3\frac{1}{2}$ times your income. The snag is that the capital you owe (the mortgage amount) is *not* fixed but goes up in line with inflation. When you come to sell, therefore, your mortgage is likely to be much higher than when you bought.

Advantage: Low monthly payments at beginning
Snag: Uncertainty about how much you will have to
pay back when you sell the house
Could be risky.

Pension Mortgage

This is available chiefly to people who are self-employed or whose employers run a company scheme. In order to encourage them to save for their old age, workers get tax relief at their highest rate on annual payments they make towards their retirement pension. To use this for mortgage insurance, the house-buyer, instead of taking out an endowment policy (on which there is no tax relief), takes out a pension policy or uses an existing pension scheme. The maximum annual pension payment on which there can be tax relief is $17\frac{1}{2}$ per cent of that year's gross income (except for elderly taxpayers, who can pay even more). When a pension matures, the pensioner is entitled to take one quarter in a lump sum, leaving the rest to provide an annual pension. The idea behind a pension mortgage is for that quarter to be pledged to the lender to repay the mortgage. Whoever sells a pension mortgage to you will probably want to put the pension part with an insurance company of their choice. Make sure you approve of the insurance company – many self-employed people who have to arrange for their own pension prefer to play safe by spreading their payments among several different companies. You may also be required to take out a further policy against your dying before retirement.

Advantage: Very tax effective
     Snags: Tax relief limited to a percentage of your income
              Pension money becomes available only when you retire
              Not accepted by every lender
              Eats into your retirement pension.

Higher Loan

There is no legal restriction on how much can be borrowed to buy a house: negotiations are between borrower and lender. But tax relief is limited to the first £30,000 of mortgage, and there is no tax relief on the excess. Some companies specialize in high loans on expensive houses at favourable rates. Such loans are available only to customers whom the lenders consider well capable of maintaining the payments. The cost may be quite high: allow for an arrangement fee, interest on the mortgage, a guarantee policy if the loan is for more than 75 per cent of the value of the house, and an endowment policy. For some loans of this type there may even be short-term arrangements whereby less than the full interest is paid, on the clear understanding that the house will be sold after only a few years and the mortgage redeemed. At times of ample money the lender may offer incentives to attract your custom. A year's reduced interest may be nice to have, but do check what happens at the end of that year. These loans are not always easy to come by and are strictly for people who know how to handle money.

Unit-Linked Mortgage

You pay insurance premiums as for an endowment mortgage. Each premium is invested in unit trusts; there is no guaranteed capital sum when your policy matures. You are really playing the stock market through the medium of your insurance company, who may very well be expert investors. If they are successful, you may do better than with a conventional 'with profits' policy. But if your units do badly, you may not be able to repay your mortgage. Insurance companies therefore sometimes combine this scheme with a policy ensuring – for a monthly premium – that there will not be a deficit. Tempting for anyone who fancies the stock market without having spare money to invest.

Snags: Risky, possibly expensive
Not accepted by many building societies.

Foreign-Currency Mortgage

Instead of borrowing £x you borrow one of the 'strong' currencies, say dollars or yen. The mortgage will eventually have to be repaid in that currency. This could make sense if a sufficient portion of your capital or income is and remains in that foreign currency. If not, then such a mortgage is highly speculative. Definitely not for beginners.

Loan by Employer

Some large firms (for example, banks) offer mortgages at low rates of interest to members of their staff. From the employee's point of view an even better scheme is one whereby the employer helps with the monthly mortgage payments. The subsidy is taxable in the employee's hands but tax relief on the mortgage is not reduced by the subsidy. Such loans will either have to be repaid when the employee leaves the firm or the monthly payments will then go up to a commercial level.

Advantage: Lower monthly mortgage payments may enable you to buy a house you could not otherwise afford

Snags: Even if mortgage is cheaper than average, other outgoings are not

You may find it difficult to change jobs.

Unless you stay with the same firm till the mortgage is paid off, it is safer to buy a house within your means at normal rates of mortgage interest.

Private Loan

Mortgages can sometimes be arranged out of trust funds either within the family or through a solicitor. Unlike other mortgages, private mortgages are often given for an indefinite period. When the lenders want their money back, they give the borrower notice; the length of notice is fixed in the mortgage – usually at around six months. In the meantime the borrower pays interest on the loan. The lenders often insist on a life insurance policy on the borrower's life, as additional security for the loan.

Advantage: Can sometimes be had for a lower rate of interest within the family, or from an employer

Snags: Not easy to come by

Interest rates may be high

Lender may demand repayment at a time when you do not have and cannot raise the money to repay.

By now you probably have one or two favourites among possible mortgages. Before you take the plunge and pay for a mortgage application, here are a few points you might want to check:

Is it the *interest rate* that pleases you? If so, how long is it likely to continue? Can the lenders change the rate of interest at will? A low rate of interest offered at the start of a mortgage may not go on for long.

Do the lenders have the right to *sell* your mortgage? Even if they do not want to put up your interest unfairly, the people who buy mortgages from them might. If this happens you should at least have the right to look for another mortgage without penalty – ask your solicitor about these points.

Are the *insurance* terms particularly attractive? If so, is the amount you will receive guaranteed, or does it rely on profits? Distinguish between a quotation from an independent adviser and one linked to a particular company. The latter may offer you an excellent deal, but if the company is not doing too well, they cannot really be expected to tell you. Find out in particular whether the insurance policy guarantees to redeem the mortgage in full. If not, to what extent does the final amount depend on the company making a consistent profit? Who are the insurance company, how profitable have they been over the past twenty years? It may be prudent to cover a possible shortfall by a separate insurance policy. Remember also that even under the best endowment policy you will receive nothing until it matures, in perhaps twenty years, when money values will have changed and when you may have long ago sold the house you are now buying.

Here are some other points which might influence you:

Are any fees included in the quotation you received? (ask which fees)

Will you have to pay any fees? (many banks and brokers charge an initial fee but building societies don't)

Will your mortgage payments go up after some years? (low start)

And some reminders:

Pension mortgages get more tax relief than others.

The policy most warmly recommended is not necessarily the best one for you.

For many people either a repayment mortgage with a protection policy or a low cost endowment mortgage are best buys.

Nevertheless, full endowment mortgages have advantages and snags for some people:

Advantages: The policy can act as health insurance: it cannot be cancelled whatever your state of health might be in the future

Tax relief is greater than under a repayment scheme because the whole of your mortgage debt remains outstanding

Insurance premiums are comparatively low for young borrowers

Life insurance continues even if you sell the house.

Snags: Premiums continue even when you have sold the house

The surrender value of the policy may be small

If the mortgage interest rate goes up, monthly payments will have to go up too – the mortgage term is not easily extended

The profits element in a 'with profits' policy is based on hope: there is no guarantee of profit. Clearly, if you opt for a type of insurance linked with investment in shares or unit trusts, there is even less guarantee.

As you can see, there is not one best buy for everyone. Your age, your health, your capital, your prospects, even your temperament, all need to be taken into consideration. So start by working out how much money you want to borrow (read Chapter 5 on what it costs to buy and run a house). Then see a bank, building society or mortgage company and ask whether they envisage any difficulty in lending that amount. If they are happy, try to get a 'mortgage certificate' – a letter saying they will lend you £x on a suitable house or flat. This useful piece of paper may help later on if several people are after the house of your desires.

Before you commit yourself, go to a different institution and put the same questions. Finally, if you are wise, you will take all the different proposals and talk them over with your solicitor (see Chapter 8).

Chapter 5

The Cost of Buying and Running a House

'House for Sale. Immaculate condition. £   . 90 per cent mortgage available.'

This kind of advertisement is meant to warm your heart. It might signal the house you can afford though your savings are slender. For a deposit of a mere ten per cent you will be able to buy a house which will almost certainly increase its value quickly. What is more you can take twenty or twenty-five years to pay for it.

Before you rush out, however, read to the end of the chapter and do your sums. Remember the '90 per cent mortgage available' means available only to someone whose income, in the eyes of a potential lender, is high enough to justify such a large loan. This was explained in Chapter 3. Against that, if finding the deposit is a problem, you may be able to borrow in excess of 90 per cent, though at a price – see Chapter 9 on deposits and Chapter 4 on different kinds of mortgage.

There will also be other expenses, such as stamp duties, valuation fees, land registry fees, legal fees, surveys and more besides. In addition, there is the cost of running the home: the more you borrow on mortgage, the higher this will be.

Do not let this chapter depress you. It is full of figures which, however you look at them, show that it costs a great deal of money to buy a house and that, when you have bought it, it will be expensive to run. Few people in the long run are happy in a tent, caravan or houseboat, or in a shared flat – therefore sooner or later they buy a house. Even though average first-time house-owners may well spend a third or more of their income on mortgage payments alone, the strain gets less as income goes up. By and large, a house usually proves a good investment. Its great charm is that inflation helps the person with the mortgage. Interest rates may go up by one or two per cent every now and then; incomes tend to go up by more. And there is tax relief on the interest payment. A mortgage up to £30,000 on the house in which you live gets tax relief at your highest personal tax rate. What is more, the mortgage itself (the money you borrowed) should not go up at all.

You are unlikely to have the courage to buy a house knowing that tomorrow you will become redundant, *but* your savings are probably better invested in a house than in a bank. For one thing, if you have to put up with prolonged unemployment you will not become eligible for social security benefits while the bulk of your capital is intact. If it is invested in a house, on the other hand, the DSS will eventually come in on your mortgage payments. Also, your chances of earning money are increased if you have a house: you might take in lodgers or start a new business from your home.

The value of your house will probably keep step with inflation. Even if you have to sell at a time when prices are steady, you will probably find that the house you are buying has not gone up either. This book is not intended for budding financiers but for people who need a home: however expensive and complicated it looks, a home is likely to be the best buy you will make in a lifetime. But try not to over-commit yourself. And choose as carefully as you can. Houses can develop expensive faults; streets and whole areas go out of fashion; health or employment can go wrong.

The first part of this chapter goes into the cost of buying a house and ends with an estimate. When you have filled in this estimate you will be able to calculate how much of your money to put into the house and how much to borrow on mortgage.

Get some idea of who will lend you that sum and on what terms. There is much more about mortgages in Chapters 3 and 4.

The second part of the chapter gives you an idea of what it will cost to run the house. Obviously, you can spend more; I am talking only of the essential running cost: the expenses you have to meet as owner. This part is unlikely to be of direct interest to your employer, but it will give you an idea of the kind of income you need to keep up the home you have in mind.

Even if you are fortunate and can get a cheap mortgage
through your employers it is worth doing your sums carefully. Paul and his wife Anthea both worked for a bank
which offered cheap mortgages to staff. They bought a most
glamorous house, relying on a low interest rate. All was fine
until five years later they were the proud parents of two
small children, Anthea was earning nothing and Paul found
he could not cope with mortgage, outgoings on his expensive
house, hire purchase payments on his car and the needs of
his young family. He required a very much better-paid job
but no such job was on hand. He concluded, rather late in
the day, that he would have done better to stick to a house
within his means.

The Cost of Buying

Capital Contribution

You won't necessarily be able to borrow all the money it takes
to buy a house. Most lending institutions insist on your putting
in some of your own. For your first house this 'capital contribution' – the difference between the price and the mortgage –
may well take up all your savings. Once you have a house to
sell when you buy another, it tends to get easier.

Some points to bear in mind:

the usual practice is for 10 per cent of the house price to be
paid by the time you exchange contracts (more about contracts
on p. 136) and the balance on completion of the purchase;

when you are selling one house to buy another, 10 per cent
of the price may have to be paid before you have access to any
of the money from your old home. If this is a problem, tell your
solicitor as soon as possible;

the capital contribution is probably your largest single payment; nevertheless, do not forget to allow for all the other
payments to be made when you buy a house. Make sure you
have enough money available.

Legal Fees

Buyer's Solicitor

There is no fixed scale of solicitor's fees. However, since many buyers are anxious to budget as tightly as possible, solicitors do their best to quote a fee at the beginning of a transaction.

Some of the newer lenders offer package deals which include legal fees. Check all your figures to see whether this would represent a real saving. If not, there is much to be said for choosing your own solicitor: if you are paying professionals to look after your interests *you* want to be the one to whom they are responsible. If their boss is a building society or a mortgage company you may, rightly or wrongly, wonder whose interests they are looking after.

On the other hand you may be lucky and get a lender who offers to add all fees to the mortgage so that you can pay them off over a period rather than at the beginning. This can be well worth accepting.

It is important not to be dazzled by the promise of low conveyancing costs until you know whether they include:

legal fees of buying;
legal fees for mortgage;
VAT on legal fees;
search fees;
Land Registry fees*;
stamp duties*;
any other fees or moneys paid out on your behalf – solicitors call them 'disbursements'.

The next few pages explain which of these fees apply to your house.

The legal fees of buying are generally somewhere below 1 per cent of the house price. But, since the amount of work to be done does not depend only on the price of the house, the percentage may well be lower for a more expensive house than for a cheaper one. Also, some solicitors will cut their fee to the minimum to give you a low quotation. They will obviously not be able to spend as much time on your particular problems – an owner who hustles you or who delays, a completion date which needs changing at the last moment –

*Not payable on every house (see p. 62).

as the firm which allows itself a more generous margin. Some publicity has been given to the computerization of conveyancing. This should help to avoid spelling errors and to shorten routine work, but I doubt whether it has much effect on the things worth paying for: the listening ear, professional advice and solutions to your particular problems. More about these in Chapter 8.

As a general rule, the lawyer dealing with a house with unregistered title has to do more work and to take greater responsibility: he has to guarantee that all is well, whereas a registered title is guaranteed by the State. To give an example: H.M. Land Registry knows the name of the owner of every piece of registered land in the country, thus making it easy for your lawyer to find out whether you are buying from the real owner. With unregistered land this can be more difficult: it is always possible for a crook to type out a deed showing himself to be the owner of Buckingham Palace, but you would not be safe to buy Buckingham Palace on the strength of that deed!

Apart from seeing to it that you buy from the right person, your solicitor has to make sure that you buy the right house and that you will be able to use it for the purpose for which you want it. A house on a new estate, though the title may be registered, tends to attract a great deal of paper – Deeds of Covenant, Deeds of Variation, Policies of Indemnity, Memorandum and Articles of Association, Planning Permission, Assignment of National House-Building Agreement, to name but a few. Some new housing developments change the neighbourhood completely: three old houses may easily become twenty-nine new flats – if you buy one of them you want to be assured that you will be able to enjoy it in peace. All this needs time, skill and care on the part of your solicitor, which may be reflected in the fees.

Mortgagee's Solicitor

Anyone lending money on mortgage will first want a solicitor to make sure that all is well with the title to the house. Ask, when you first inquire about a mortgage, whether the lending organization will instruct your own solicitor to do the legal work. If yes, this fee will be low, as there is not usually a lot of extra work involved. If no, check with the lenders whether you will be charged separately. Also, whenever a lender offers free conveyancing or 'inclusive of legal fees' find out whether they mean your fees for buying or their own fees for lending, and whether they mean all fees, or only some of them.

Inspection Fee

No financial institution lends money unless its surveyor has seen the house and advised on whether the house will sell and repay your mortgage should you default. Fees depend on the price of the house, not on the amount you want to borrow, and vary slightly between lenders.

Lending Fee or Accommodation Fee

This fee is not charged by building societies, nor by all banks. It is mentioned here to alert you to an expense which you may be able to avoid if you have a choice of possible lenders. Ask the lender well before you sign on the dotted line. Some offers, particularly of mortgages difficult to obtain elsewhere, are accompanied by very high fees.

Guarantee Policy

Another expense which you may or may not have to meet. If your mortgage is above 80 per cent you will almost certainly be required to take out this insurance and pay a single premium for it. But if you are lucky it will be added to your mortgage debt.

Local Authority Search Fee

This fee could be less than £20 for a postal search made by your solicitors to an authority which replies speedily. But some are so slow (or so overworked or short of staff) that it becomes necessary to make a personal search. You can do this yourself, but it may be safer to let your solicitors send specialist agents. Your solicitors can advise on this and tell you how much the agents would charge.

Land Registry Fees

As soon as you have bought a house with unregistered title in an area of compulsory registration, all the title deeds have to be sent to the Land Registry for the preparation of a land certificate (or charge certificate). Council houses bought by sitting tenants under the Housing Act 1980 must be registered, wherever they may be. The fee depends on the amount you pay for the house. The following table gives some examples:

Price of House:	£20,001 −£25,000	£40,001 −£45,000	£60,001 −£70,000	£100,001 −£150,000
Land registry fee:	£30	£60	£100	£160

Stamp Duty

Normally there is no stamp duty on a house or flat bought for £30,000 or less. Houses or flats costing over £30,000 are subject to stamp duty at 1 per cent. Thus, on a house costing exactly £30,000 you pay no stamp duty, but at £30,100 the stamp duty is £301; at £40,000 it is £400, at £50,000 it is £500, etc. There may be additional stamp duty if you are buying a house on a new lease (see below).

One reason why your solicitors are likely to collect all these fees from you before the house purchase is completed is that there are strict time limits. If documents are not stamped or sent to the Land Registry in time there are penalties to pay and you lose protection.

Stamp Duty on a New Lease

Let us suppose you buy a new flat for £25,000, with a lease for 120 years at a ground rent of £25 for the first thirty years (which is all you are likely to be concerned about as you intend to stay only a few years), the rent doubling every thirty years thereafter.

There is no stamp duty on the £25,000 (see above). But you have to pay stamp duty on the average rent (£93.75) calculated over the whole period of the lease.

To give some examples:

Stamp duty			
Average yearly rent	£10	£50	£100
Lease for 99 years	£1.20	£6.00	£12.00
Lease for over 100 years	£2.40	£12.00	£24.00

Beware of an average yearly rent of more than £300. It attracts stamp duty on the purchase price, however low.

There may also be an additional small Land Registry fee.

Other Fees

There will be other, minor, fees. Some solicitors charge separately for postage and telephones, others include these in their fees. Allow also for VAT.

Going through the above points you can check whether you can afford to buy the house of your choice.

To borrow, in spite of unusually high expense, may make good sense; but, before you commit yourself, do make an estimate.

Your estimated cost
Capital
Inspection fee*
Solicitor's fee*   house
                          mortgage
Land Registry fee   house
Stamp duty   house
Other fees
Removal*
Survey*

_____

£

_____

*Add VAT to all these items.

Check whether you have been told of other fees, for example accommodation fees; if so, are you entering into a good bargain? And do not overlook the running fees dealt with in the next few pages.

If at this point you come to the view that you simply cannot afford the kind of home you had in mind, what can you do? Here are some ideas to try:

(1) Look in a different road
in a different district
for a smaller house
for an older house.

(2) Look for a better-paid job.

(3) Consider whether evening classes could help you to qualify for a better job.

(4) Try other mortgage lenders, but see below for a warning.

(5) Consider whether you can add to your income in other ways (e.g. by working extra time, doing part-time minicab driving, cleaning or decorating).

(6) Consider adding to your present house instead of moving.

(7) Try to find a flat under a shared ownership scheme (more about this on p. 125).

(8) Look into the possibility of renting, using a housing association, or sharing with somebody else (for most of us these last three possibilities are not very hopeful).

Perhaps you feel you can afford the house and the running of it, but you cannot raise a big enough mortgage. If so, can you increase your capital by doing some extra work as suggested above, or by letting a room, or by living with mother for a while? These, I realize, are desperate remedies, but they are only temporary and they will allow you to put money by – if you are strong-minded.

Or you could try to get a bigger loan: but look carefully at any increased offers. Unconventional lenders often charge a good deal more than ordinary building societies. If the loan means higher monthly payments you may be worse off in the long run. As has been mentioned, some lenders charge a fee for introducing business or insist on your taking out an insurance policy which may or may not be useful to you.

The Cost of Running a Home

Mortgage Payments

Repayment mortgages are paid off by instalments; endowment mortgages are paid off in one lump sum at the end of the mortgage period. Payments of interest and of endowment insurance premium (or, in the case of repayment mortgages, of interest and a slice of capital) are usually made monthly. On very high mortgages, though, payments often come half-yearly or once a year. You may find it most convenient to tell your bank to make these payments by standing order without your having to tell them every time. All you need is a form saying how much to pay, on what day and to whom. The bank does the rest.

In your budget, allow for interest to go up or down. When interest rates change, your payments may also change. Unless the bank has your authority to pay whatever is demanded, standing orders may need altering from time to time. In any event, remember to put enough money into the bank. If you have an expensive second mortgage or bank loan it is well worth asking the first mortgagee after a time whether it will increase your first mortgage to allow you to pay off the expensive additional loan. If they agree, your monthly payments can come down a good way.

Ground Rent

In some parts of the country freehold houses attract a payment of rent, usually called 'chief rent'. Leasehold houses and flats are always liable to ground rent. Apart from these exceptions there is no need to allow for rent.

Insurance

Endowment or Top-Up Insurance Policy
Ordinary life insurance is beyond the scope of this book. You may find, however, that you cannot get the mortgage you need to buy the house without taking out some kind of insurance maturing at the end of your mortgage or on your death.

There has been an enormous increase in the number of endowment insurance policies. Some of them offer very good terms, others are expensive, speculative or both. Get several quotations from different firms if you possibly can, as advised in previous chapters. Higher monthly payments do not always guarantee more money in the long run.

Mortgage Protection Policy

A mortgage protection policy costs a good deal less than an ordinary life policy, because its purpose is much more limited: it does no more than repay the mortgage if you should die before you have paid it off. If you survive to the end of the mortgage period, you stop paying insurance premiums, but you get nothing. For a slightly higher premium you can insure the mortgage plus a sum of money at the end of the mortgage term. This type of insurance is comparatively inexpensive, particularly if you are young when you take it out; at the same time it is a comfort in case the breadwinner should die. A form of mortgage protection policy is also used for part of the 'low cost' endowment insurance (p. 46).

House

To insure the house against fire and other common risks is common sense. When there is a mortgage on the house, the lenders (building society, bank or insurance company) insist on house insurance, usually through their agency. You should, however, be given a reasonable choice of insurance companies. When the house or flat you buy is leasehold, the owner of the freehold often makes the right to handle the insurance of the building a term of the lease. The mortgagee usually gives way and allows the freeholder to insure. This is sensible: a leasehold house or flat is usually one of several in the same block or road. If some flats are damaged the insurance claim is more easily dealt with by one insurance company than by several. House insurance premiums are fairly reasonable. There is more about house insurance in Chapter 14.

Furniture, etc.

It is in your own interest to insure the contents of your house. It is also easy to forget, because no building society, solicitor or insurance agent is likely to push the right form in front of you at the right moment. The right moment is as soon as you own the stuff: it could be stolen or burnt the very next day. You can, but don't have to, insure with the company which insures your house. See what different insurance companies have to offer before you choose. Unless you are told differently, the ordinary contents policy covers your goods only for their value at the time of the disaster, which may be a good deal less than it costs to replace them. Therefore, go for an index-linked policy offering to replace your belongings, if you can afford it.

Many policies exclude money above £50 or £100 (unless you pay an extra premium); for a comparatively small additional premium you can also insure your jewellery, sports equipment, the contents of your freezer, etc.

Some companies offer to reduce the premium if you have secure doors and special window locks. Not everyone is fond of these devices: some people fear that window locks make escape more difficult in case of fire. A burglar alarm or membership of a Neighbourhood Watch Scheme commend themselves to some insurance companies. So, as in other respects, it is worth asking a few people for quotations before deciding on insurance.

Rates and Water Rates

The community charge (or poll tax) will shortly replace domestic rates. Your liability to community charge does not depend on whether you are a houseowner. Water rates will probably continue. For details apply to the local authority.

There are other outgoings. How much you will have to allow for them depends partly on taste, partly on luck. In any case you should bear them in mind. Here are some examples:

Repairs

If you are wise you will have had the house surveyed (see Chapter 10, 'Surveyors') before you bought it and will have a rough idea of its condition. An old house bought at a low price will probably need more extensive repairs than a new one.

You should know about the likelihood of settlement, the need for roof repairs and the presence of rot and woodworm, before you move. It is possible that the mortgagees may specify repairs which have to be done before they will lend money on a house, or they may hold back part of the mortgage money till these repairs have been carried out. Requirements of this kind are included in the mortgage offer, so you can plan accordingly. Your surveyor may also be able to give you a rough idea of how much to allow for routine maintenance per year. In addition there are bound to be unexpected repairs, though some of these may be covered by insurance (see above).

Painting and papering the inside of the house will take more or less money depending on how often you decorate and whether you do the work yourself or have it done professionally. A room which is well lived in will probably need repainting every three years or so.

Service Charge

The lease of a flat in a modern block will probably say that major repairs and maintenance will be done for you and that you will have to share the cost. Sometimes central heating or hot water are provided in this way; or there may be a caretaker who cleans the stairs and looks after the garden. All such expenses are usually called 'service charge'. Ask the present owner how much he has had to pay each year and what his service charge includes. This will give you an idea of how much to allow under this heading. If the cost of major repairs to the building is included in the service charge you can allow a smaller sum under the heading 'repairs'.

Fares

As a rule, houses near the centre of a town are more expensive than those further out, though fashionable suburbs may be dearer than run-down areas further in. You may have to decide whether you prefer to spend more on a house near your place of work and less on fares, or the other way round. Bear in mind that fares tend to go up rather more frequently than mortgage rates, and allow for time spent on travelling to and from work.

If you have a car, can you park at your place of work? If your house has no garage, will the car depreciate too fast? Opinions vary, and so do cars. Weigh against the price of renting a garage the possibility of having to pay parking fees, and possibly parking fines.

Shops, Domestic Help, etc.

Your cost of living goes up if you have an expensive journey to good shops, or if the shops near you are expensive. Prices can vary considerably even between one part of a suburb and another. The presence of a supermarket or two will probably mean shopping at reasonable prices.

Domestic help is not only more expensive but also more difficult to find in more 'select' areas. It is equally difficult to find in areas where there are many factories offering part-time employment. If you depend on the help of a cleaner this point is worth remembering.

Lifestyle

The cost of your social life does not necessarily depend on the area where you live. A hermit can live independently of others. But the chances are that if everyone in the road has a Jaguar you may not long feel happy with your own Mini, and even if you do, your partner might not, and the children will most certainly wish to do just as everyone else in their school or street. It is worth peering through the neighbours' windows before finally deciding on the house. You may feel equally uncomfortable if yours is the Jaguar and the neighbours go about in elderly bone-shakers.

Jot down the figures as they come, and then work out how much to allow per month. For example, if insurance is £150 per half-year, allow £25 per month; if fares are £1 a day and you work a five-day week, allow 22 working days per month, or £22.

If you are paid weekly, you may find it useful to make a

weekly budget rather than a monthly one. But in any event, don't assume that because you have a little over in one month you will not need it during the following month.

Estimated cost of running your house

Outgoing	Cost per year		Total per month
Mortgage	£	per year	£
(Ground rent or chief rent)	£	(per year)	£
Insurance			
House	£	per year	£
Contents	£	per year	£
Mortgage	£	per year	£
Rates*	£	per half year	£
Water rate	£	per half year	£
Fares	£	per day/week	£
Repairs/service charge	£	per year	£

*Until they are replaced by the community charge.

Chapter 6

Estate Agents

Estate agents are very much caught up in the supermarket idea of house-buying mentioned in Chapter 1. Hundreds of old established firms have quietly taken down their facia boards and replaced them with new ones: Property Services, Financial Services, One Stop Estate Agents – all sorts of wonderful names appear in large letters, and their own in small ones. 'For Sale' signs outside houses have undergone a similar transformation. The change may be to your advantage, because you may get as much help with house-buying as before, plus, if you wish, suggestions for a mortgage and insurance. On the other hand, a firm with a very similar facia board may be run by insurance brokers with estate agency as a sideline. The difference may not be easy to detect at first glance. So, remember to concentrate on houses, and if you don't get much response, go elsewhere.

If you have followed the advice in previous chapters you will have come across estate agents through newspaper advertisements. You will again meet estate agents when you visit the area where you are looking for a house. Some of the newer firms are in the high streets, but traditionally estate agents are attracted to railway stations like pins to a magnet. Look in their windows. Even if you do not see what you want, a visit can do no harm. Many agents are happy to put every inquirer on their list.

The agent will ask how much you want to spend on the house, whether you want a mortgage and for how much, how many rooms you want, whether you need a garage and whether you have a particular area in mind. You may think all manner of other things are important, but these are the ones that matter to agents and will decide what information they will send you in the future. In my experience it is pretty useless to tell an agent that you want, for example, a house to which another room can be added, or one facing in a particular direction – their indexing system is rarely geared to picking out this kind of information.

The amount of mortgage will have to do with the kind of house which agents bring to your notice. You might enjoy living in a converted windmill, but you won't be able to borrow 95 per cent of the purchase price on mortgage for anything other than a conventionally built house or flat.

While you are with the agents, they may suggest a few houses which you can visit then and there. No reputable agent will ask you to sign any document, so regard any suggestion of this kind with suspicion. Agents are often very helpful merely in the hope of showing you the house of your choice or of doing other business with you; you are under no obligation either to buy or to pay them a fee.

If the estate agent has nothing suitable to offer on the spot, they will nevertheless put your name on their mailing list. If you have to come from some distance to look at houses, they may be able to arrange for you to see several on your next visit. In the meantime you will be receiving sheaves of literature from them if this is a quiet time of year. If you are house-hunting in the middle of a season of panic-buying, on the other hand, all the running will have to be made by you. Concentrate on one or two agents, or you will lose your sanity – and keep your eyes open for other possibilities.

If at all feasible, get familiar with the problems of house-hunting during the quiet season.

The language used by estate agents can itself be a challenge. Some agents indulge in amusing description, making ordinary houses sound fun to live in. This is all to the good, so long as you remember that you will have to live in the ordinary house long after you have forgotten the fanciful description. The majority of agents use words which the house-hunter may at first find bewildering. What, for example, should you make of a 'residence with two reception rooms and a well-kept garden'? Before the vision of a stately-home-to-be runs away with you and you to rush out to buy, you would do well to keep your head and begin to understand some of the language used by estate agents.

There is little difference between a 'house', a 'residence' and a 'property'. A 'residence' tends to be slightly larger and draughtier than a 'property', though a 'bijou residence' is likely to be very small indeed. A 'period style' residence probably means either mock Georgian or mock Tudor. 'Ready for modernization', 'old-world charm' or 'fully modernized' should warn you that the building needs a careful survey. 'Panoramic view' may mean 'very windy'; 'close to city centre' could be very noisy. A semi-detached house has three outside walls to look after; a detached house has four. Detached houses, even if built close together, tend to fetch higher prices, terraced houses (attached on both sides) tend to go for less, except for modern 'town houses', or houses in a genuine period terrace. Bungalows do not usually present any mortgage problems, but houses with part possession do. Building societies do not usually take kindly to a house part of which is occupied by a sitting tenant.

The great majority of houses offered for sale are built on two floors. Agents usually call any room on the first floor a bedroom and on the ground floor a reception room. 'Reception room' does not mean that it will be large enough for receptions; it is merely a word for 'living room', though an upstairs room may have a pleasant view, get more sun and make an altogether better living room than those on the ground floor. An 'integral garage' cannot necessarily be reached from inside the house. A 'master bedroom' indicates that there is at least one other bedroom, even smaller. A 'double bedroom' will be large enough to hold a double bed. In some modern flats, however, there may not be enough space to get in and out of that bed on both sides, or to add items of luxury such as a wardrobe. A built-in wardrobe might be worth two feet of space, particularly if it has sliding doors. The agents' particulars will probably include approximate measurements for each room. Bear in mind that size alone does not always give a clear picture. Some new dwellings are marvels of planning and use space most ingeniously. This could mean that you could do without a lot of furniture, because much is built in, or that you can make do with a place smaller than you had thought possible because, for example, the built-in breakfast counter extends to make a dining table. But not every modern house is well planned.

'Bathroom en suite' could mean that you cannot reach a WC except by going through the main bedroom. For such a house you need a second lavatory.

Modern kitchens are often referred to as 'kitchenettes'; a room with nothing but a sink is called a 'scullery' in an old house and a 'utility room' in a new house. A 'patio' may mean a delightful paved garden area, or a dreary back yard. A 'study' will probably be designed for a studious dwarf.

A word about flats and maisonettes. 'Maisonnette' is French for a 'small house'; in modern English the word is usually spelt with one 'n' and betokens never more than part of a house. Neither 'flat' nor 'maisonette' is a very exact term, though most agents and property developers talk of a 'flat' if it is reached through a common entrance, shared by the occupiers of other flats. A modern 'maisonette', on the other hand, is usually reached by its own staircase if on the first floor, and direct from the outside if on the ground floor. Older maisonettes are sometimes on two floors, modern maisonettes more often on one floor. A 'studio flat' will have only one room plus (with luck) a kitchen, bath and WC. A 'penthouse' is high up and very expensive.

People with very different qualifications carry on business as estate agents. An agent may have qualified after a course in estate management and years of professional training; he or she may specialize in selling houses and goods by auction, in letting flats, in collecting rents, or in making valuations. Some agents are less concerned with professional skills than with the business of selling houses, with the result that there are firms without a single professionally qualified member. This is no reflection on their skill or their ability to help a house-hunter.

Whatever their professional qualifications, or even if they have no professional qualifications, estate agents can be extremely useful to the house-buyer. For one thing, they are likely to know more about houses for sale in their area than anyone else. In some areas all agents cooperate and exchange lists, so that it is enough to see one in order to hear of all the houses in the district. But this is by no means universal, and it is quite a good idea for you to visit two or three agents in one area in order to hear about as many houses as possible. At the same time be warned and do not buy merely on the strength of a first impression. Look at houses similar to the one you are interested in; you will then be able to judge how their price and condition compare.

The very friendliness and helpfulness of an estate agent sometimes leads buyers astray. Agents are employed by the *owner* of a house to sell that house. They must not give you a misleading description of the house, but it is not their function to warn a buyer of its defects. Indeed, they may well be failing in their duty to the seller if they did warn you. It is therefore up to you to be wary.

Keep firmly in mind that your main purpose is to buy a house, and that you went to see estate agents to find out whether they could show you suitable houses. If an agent, incidentally, suggests a good mortgage, fine. But it is for *you* to make sure it is suitable. Read the chapters on mortgages, then get quotations as suggested. Compare them carefully. Be wary of any suggestion that the house is available only to people who also buy a particular mortgage linked with a particular insurance policy. The insurance element of such a package deal may not be to your advantage. Do not forget to look separately at house, mortgage and insurance. If the agent produces an attractive insurance offer, ask all the questions suggested in earlier chapters. Remember that you are a potential buyer, not just of a house but of a mortgage and of an insurance policy. Even if you decide against buying one of the houses on their list, you are worth wooing as a customer. Do not be afraid of showing that you know what you are about.

Part 2

The House You Want

Chapter 7

Meeting the Owner and Making Sure

Before you meet *the* owner, you will have met a great many owners of a great many houses. This is as it should be: you would be unwise to buy the first house you see without also inspecting others. However good this first house may look to you, take time to read local papers and to visit the area, as recommended in earlier chapters. Be particularly wary of two points:

The price: Although this house may be a lot cheaper than a similar house you saw earlier in the week in another area, do not jump to the conclusion that you are on to a bargain. House prices vary extraordinarily, not only from one part of the country to another, but even from one part of the city to another. Even within the same suburb you may find two similar houses offered at different prices. Before you rush in to buy the lower priced house, make sure that it really is a bargain: consider its age and condition, and, above all, compare it with other houses in the immediate neighbourhood.

The future: If the house really seems a bargain, check that its future is relatively safe. Maybe the price has come down because of a road-widening scheme, or because there are plans for a new airport round the corner. A visit to the local town hall and to the local pub will probably yield information on these points. Teetotallers might try a local shop – not of course self-service; a nice, slow, old-fashioned shop lends itself to conversation and is often visited by old residents who will, at the drop of a hint, shake their heads about what the neighbourhood is coming to. This is precisely what you want to know: what *is* the neighbourhood coming to? But, as with pub information, take it with a pinch of salt and check with the local council. The chief use of local gossip is that it gives you an idea of what questions to ask of the council.

Gaining experience involves not only looking at local papers but also walking round many houses. After a time you will be able to recognize within two minutes the house you do *not* want. You are then in difficulty. Should you tour the house, wasting a lot of time, yours and the owner's, and leave, mumbling 'I'll let you know'? Or should you take a look at the house and retire hurriedly, leaving the owner waiting and wondering?

To my mind it is a reasonable compromise to inspect at least two rooms to make sure your impression was correct, and then to end the inspection with a reasonable excuse which will not deflate the owner too much. 'I'm afraid it will be too difficult to get my grandmother's wheelchair up the stairs' is better than 'The view from the back window is too depressing for words'. Remember that owners are human. If you have made an appointment and cannot keep it, let them know. They may have stayed at home to show you the house, or they may have gone there specially to meet you: they deserve an apology, even if you do not like the house or are too weary to make the trip.

Let us assume you have reached the dizzy point when you like the house and the view from the house, and it comes within the price range you can afford.

Take another long cool look.

Are the windows double-glazed? Do they open easily? Is the attic insulated? How about draughts? If there is central heating, is it in every room?

Perhaps the house is beautifully painted and papered, all floors covered with fitted carpets and vinyl tiles, the whole thing spotless and well cared for. How marvellous to move in without having to decorate! But it is as well to allow for the possibility that the house was newly decorated in order to hide cracks under the paper and rot under the tiles. A surveyor will be able to tell.

Conversely, do not be put off by the owners' ghastly taste; old paint and ugly wallpaper can be removed. And the awful curtains and greasy mats will leave with them. It is quite possible that you will be able to buy the house at a much lower price than one that was recently dolled up. The owners may have paid all of two thousand pounds for the house some thirty years ago and feel that they are making a splendid profit.

Whether or not you share the owners' tastes, try to imagine the house with all furniture removed, and refurnish it in your mind. Imagine your family moving round the house. The back room, dark now because the curtains are drawn and the sun is at the front, will get the afternoon sun and would take Granny's large wardrobe. The washing machine could go to the right of the sink. The stairs are a little steep for your toddler, but she won't be a toddler much longer and you can fix a gate at the top of the stairs.

It is a little difficult if, while you are busy imagining, you also have to cope with talkative owners, bent on explaining every advantage of the house. You may find it best to listen to them on your first round, and then ask to go round once more. If they insist on tagging along, ignore their further remarks and concentrate. You can come out of your trance every now and then and explain with an apologetic smile: 'I am so sorry, I did not hear what you said. I am trying very hard to remember everything about the house so that I can tell my wife/husband all about it. Do you mind if I continue?'

Do not allow your irritation with the owners to colour your impression of the house. They will go, taking with them their noisy children and revolting pets. It is not safe to assume that, because they are awful, your new neighbours are going to be like them. They may have been the scourge of the neighbourhood and the neighbours may all be watching and praying behind their curtains that they will go and you will buy. Equally, do not let charming owners with impeccable taste and beautiful furniture persuade you to buy an unsuitable house. They too will go, leaving you to do the best you can with your sagging three-piece suite and the carpet with the hole at the centre.

Use all your senses. Do not only look at the house, listen for traffic, factories, schools, railways, birds, music. You will get some idea of what to expect. If possible, pay several calls at different times of the day. Your nose also has its part to play. The delicious smell of roses or lilac may give you a quite illusory air of luxury. And the fusty smell of cats, or not enough windows open, may put you off. (On this I speak with feeling: my family refused a house because the owner bred, and did not clean up after, a very large number of cats. Nothing I could say persuaded them that the cats would leave and the smell evaporate.) But a bad smell may be bad drains or dry rot – a surveyor should be able to tell the difference!

It is important to use your imagination when looking at a house, but it is as well to keep your feet on the ground. Not every old cowshed converts into a dream cottage. Many derelict buildings are in that state because it would cost too much to put them right. Not every old house lends itself to modernization: some are the wrong shape for modern furniture, and the money it would take to convert is better employed in buying a more expensive house in the first place. On the other hand, four sound walls and a good roof may give a lot of scope for improvement without financial ruin. If you are thinking of converting a shed, church or railway station, get a builder or architect to look at it before you commit yourself. Also, find out whether you could get a local authority grant and whether you need planning permission for the change.

Some Pitfalls

Your Offer Letter

When you have made up your mind to buy the house, you will want the owners to know as soon as possible – indeed, you are probably anxious in case they sell to somebody else. By all means tell them you would like to buy the house, that you are at once applying for a mortgage and that they will be hearing from your solicitors. But take care: Chapter 13 explains in more detail that neither the buyer nor the seller of a house is bound to go on with the sale until they exchange contracts. It also explains why you cannot safely enter into a contract till you know a good deal more about the house. You must therefore be careful not to bind yourself unwittingly. Your letter to the owner, however friendly, may amount to the 'written evidence' which in law can make the difference between a tentative offer and a binding contract.* Whether you talk to the owner or whether you write, make it clear that

*There is talk of changing the law on this point.

your offer is SUBJECT TO CONTRACT. You could write something like this:

Letter to owner

Dear Mr Smith

Thank you for letting me see the house again on Sunday. We liked it very much and hope to make a formal offer for it. I am going to see the building society tomorrow, and have made an appointment with my solicitors for Thursday. I am asking them to write to you, or if you can let me have the name and address of your own solicitors before Thursday I shall ask mine to get in touch with yours.

Yours sincerely,

This letter, without committing you, tells the owner that you are serious about his house. In times of shortage you can say the same thing more emphatically – but you must still take care not to commit yourself. If you have prepared your visit, you might be able to write:

As I told you we already have a mortgage certificate. I am asking the brokers today how soon I can expect the money. I am also telling my solicitors to go ahead, and shall be in touch with you as soon as I have the mortgage. In the meantime I have given my solicitor a preliminary deposit to send on to your solicitors.

It may be that you want to explore whether the owner will reduce the price and do not want to go to a solicitor till you know whether you will be able to afford the house. In that case, if you follow the wording of the next letter fairly closely (leaving out what does not apply), you are safe. But do not use phrases like 'I am offering', or 'Will you take'.

Letter to owner

Dear Mr Smith

Thank you for letting us see the house again on Sunday. We liked it very much and hope to make a formal offer. Would you consider £   , subject to contract, the price to include the vinyl in bathroom, kitchen and hall, and all fittings?*

I am sorry I cannot offer the full price, but as you know, the house

*Or whatever else the owner has told you would be included in the sale for no extra payment. If nothing was said, leave this part of the sentence out.

will need complete repainting and the bathroom modernizing. If you are prepared to sell the house to me, please give me the name and address of your solicitors. I shall ask my solicitors to get in touch with them.

Yours sincerely,

If you saw the house through an estate agent, there is no need to write to the owner at all. Telephone the agents instead and ask them to contact the owner. You can at the same time mention to them any defects which you feel might persuade the owner to lower the price. Even without defect, the owner may well be prepared to lower the price; most house prices are fixed with the idea of dropping the price a little if need be. If there is no urgency, you could write:

Letter to an estate agent

Dear Sir,

re: 14 Chestnut Avenue

Would you please find out whether the owner is willing to sell this house for £   , subject to contract. I think the price at which it is offered is rather high: the house needs repainting and the bathroom is very old-fashioned. I have spoken to the   Building Society who are willing to give me a mortgage. As soon as I hear from you that my offer is acceptable, I shall make a formal application. My solicitors are Stokes & Stokes of

Yours faithfully,

If you have already been to your solicitors and discussed the purchase with them, you can ask your solicitor to put forward the offer. This is particularly convenient if you are dealing direct with the owner, without an estate agent. Write to the solicitor:

Dear Ms Stokes,

Would you please offer £   for 14 Chestnut Avenue, Bursledon, the house about which I saw you last week. The owner is Mr   . I answered his advertisement in the local paper; there is no agent involved. I do not know the name of his solicitor.

If he is prepared to sell at my price I shall send a surveyor and then apply for a mortgage.

(Or: Could you in the meantime please suggest where I should go for a mortgage of £   .) Please let me know when I should pay a deposit.

Yours sincerely

If you have not yet been to a solicitor, now is the time to go.

The Deposit

You may feel that, to stop the owner from selling the house to anybody else, you should as quickly as possible press money into his or her hands. This impulse is human, but the owner is not bound to reserve the house for you even if you pay a deposit. The owner's solicitors, once they have sent a contract to your solicitors, will not normally deal with a second applicant for the house without first sending out a warning. You cannot, however, rely on this. Therefore, do not pay a deposit direct to the owner. If you do and the sale falls through, you might have difficulty in claiming your deposit back. If you cannot resist the impulse to pay a deposit, pay through your solicitors. They will make sure that you can get it back.

Above all, do not get carried away. Do not start buying carpets or furniture. You cannot be certain of getting the house till contracts have been exchanged. If the sale falls through, even though it is no fault of yours and much to your disappointment, you can get no compensation from the owners. They are not responsible for your carpets, your hurt feelings, your building society fees or your legal costs.

This seems enormously unjust till you find yourself in the position of one of Tom's friends. Roger had fondly hoped to buy a house to go with his new job. Then he heard the new job did not offer the bright future he had been led to expect. He stayed put in his old job and his old house. The owner of the new house had been waiting for many weeks, lost the house he had hoped to buy and spent quite a bit on finding another house for his family. All this because he had relied on Roger to buy his house. Yet Roger owed him no compensation.

Gazumping

In recent years this principle of not being bound to buy or sell a house till contracts are exchanged has given more offence to buyers than to sellers. House-owners may quite enjoy showing you their property today and agreeing a price with you. They can show it to somebody else tomorrow and settle for a higher price. Till one of you signs and exchanges contracts with the owner, no one is under any liability to go on.

If you relied on the owner to sell to you, paid for a survey, applied for a mortgage, consulted a solicitor and, after some weeks, are told he or she wants more money or is selling to somebody else, you are understandably cross. No one has found a solution to this problem, though solicitors have at least made it a rule not to deal with more than one would-be buyer without letting the other know. You are, therefore, fairly safe in assuming that you are the only buyer, till your solicitors get a letter telling them the owner is dealing with somebody else.

If you are trying to buy at a time when everyone seems to be frantically house-hunting, get a mortgage certificate before you join the rush. Many lending institutions are prepared to give a certificate saying how much they are prepared to lend you on a suitable house. If the terms of the offer are good but the lenders are short of money and cannot produce the money immediately, your bank (if it is not the lender) might tide you over. Or, better still, you might persuade your bank to match the offer.

Gazumping might disappear if the Scottish system was adopted in the rest of Britain, but this would introduce new uncertainties and disadvantages. In Scotland, once your offer is accepted, you are committed to buying on a certain date. But can you be sure you will have the money ready by that date if you have not yet sold your own house? No one has yet come up with the perfect solution, though estate agents are being encouraged to oppose gazumping with more vigour than they have shown in the past.

It is possible that gazumping will be outlawed in the not too distant future. In the meantime, it is impossible to give reliable advice on this thorny subject. House prices can rise very rapidly at times, but such periods are usually followed by a lull or even a slight drop in prices. If you are not pushed for time and if you have a house to sell as well as wishing to buy, you will probably have a less frustrating time if you wait. First-time buyers, on the other hand, may fear that prices will rise much faster than their savings. They might consider camping out to queue for a newly built house on a fair-sized estate; prices tend to be fixed and gazumping is cut out.

Some builders of new housing estates offer an option: for a non-returnable deposit the house is reserved for you for a period at a fixed price. If you buy, the initial payment becomes part of the purchase money. If you don't (for example because you can't get a mortgage), you lose the deposit. This is not to be recommended unless you are virtually certain that you can buy the house, but is possibly less frustrating than the uncertainty connected with the other forms of purchasing.

At whatever time you buy, make it a rule not to discuss business with the owners. Visit them by all means, though not too often or they will worry and think that you are in doubt about whether you really want the house. Oddly enough, you are expected to make up your mind about a house, where you may spend the best part of your life, after the most cursory visits. Owners do not think this odd: they still regard the house as their own and want to go on living there undisturbed till it is sold. They will tolerate, with as much grace as can be mustered, visits from you and surveyors. The rest is better done by correspondence, via estate agents or solicitors.

Chapter 8

Help! You Need a Solicitor

Why go to a solicitor at all? Could you not save money by getting the lending institution or a licensed conveyancer to buy your house and a broker to tell you what mortgage to apply for?

The answer is yes, and again no.

It is tempting to avoid the expense and trouble of getting independent advice or of checking awkward figures which no one makes easy for you. You may prefer to hope for the best, though I imagine that if you trust luck to that extent you probably won't have read as far as this. You will never know that you have done badly.

The great advantage of talking to solicitors, not just about conveyancing but also about your proposed financial arrangements, is that solicitors tend to be enormously experienced in looking objectively at other people's plans and problems. This is sometimes overlooked in the general scramble for speed and cheapness. Solicitors themselves contribute by advertising how cheaply they can do your conveyancing.

If cheapness is your only criterion you may wish to compare the fees of solicitors with those of licensed conveyancers. Licensed conveyancers have passed exams authorizing them to deal with buying and selling houses, but their qualifications are obviously more limited than those of solicitors. Unlicensed conveyancers have not passed those exams and are not allowed to do all the work connected with house-buying. A good deal of heartache can be prevented by timely independent advice – this is a plug for my own profession, based on my own experience.

Conveyancing is a small part of what you ought to use solicitors for: I suggest you talk to them as soon as you come up against any of the following:

you are not sure which mortgage is best for you;

you intend to buy together with someone else;

you are asked to pay a deposit (see Chapter 9) or an endowment premium;

you are thinking of buying a lease, or a house with part possession, or sheltered accommodation.

Show the different insurance offers you have received to your solicitors and discuss their pros and cons.

Where to Borrow

The Financial Services Act will give you some protection (the Act has the primary aim of preventing fraud on investors), but neither a broker nor anyone else has to advise you on a choice of mortgages, and it is at present somewhat doubtful whether it is anybody's duty to advise on package deals which comprise mortgage and insurance. Solicitors will, if asked.

If in the past you have taken out loans you cannot afford, the moment before buying a house may be the time to sort yourself out. Solicitors may well be able to suggest more appropriate loans.

Unlike all others to whom you might have been talking about insurance, solicitors can assess whether you need all the insurance you have been offered without having a personal interest in your decision. They alone have to account to you for any commission they might receive if you decide to buy an insurance policy through them. This may be one reason why solicitors are able to see the good points of non-commission-paying policies, which ought to be better for you as all your money goes towards buying your policy. (This is not an immutable law – some companies are more successful at investing than others.)

Joint Purchase

Buying a house or flat is often the result of joint effort by two or more people. Couples – married or not – or several friends clubbing together to find the deposit should decide at the start how they are going to own the place. Up to four names can go on the title deeds, but since the lenders will probably consider the earnings of no more than two they may not want the others officially mentioned. Talk this over with your solicitors: they will probably suggest a simple document which says in what proportions the house is to be owned by each of the people contributing. Do not leave this until you have fallen out and nobody remembers precisely what was intended. More about joint purchase in Chapter 13.

Sheltered Housing

Some of the special problems are mentioned in Chapter 2. To avoid friction within the family it can be a good idea for everyone to understand what is likely to happen. In particular, relatives who benefit under an elderly person's will may want to know how such a purchase will affect them. They may even come up with other solutions.

Buying a Lease

A house offered on a long lease is probably as valuable as a comparable freehold house. The tail end of what was once a long lease could be a bargain if it carried with it the right to buy the freehold; it could become an expensive nightmare if at the end of the lease you had to do all the repairs left undone by previous owners.

How long is a 'long lease'? In law, any lease over twenty-one years is 'long', but you may need a very much more extensive term. Any lease which has less than seventy years to run should lead to a quick telephone call to your solicitors before you commit yourself in any way.

If you are buying a *flat* it will almost certainly be leasehold. This is no disadvantage. There is much more about flats in

Chapter 11. If you are thinking of buying a leasehold *house*, read on.

A freehold house is yours forever, a leasehold one only until the lease runs out. Lenders love freehold houses, and house-hunters who want to borrow as much money as possible are wise to look at freehold houses or very long leaseholds. The difference from the house-buyer's point of view is that a lease-hold house will cost rent each year. This rent, known as ground rent, tends to be very small and is not usually a great worry. Much more important is the fact that, in theory at least, at the end of the lease the house goes back to the owner of the ground. Leasehold houses therefore are worth less as time goes on, whereas freehold houses tend to go up in value. Building societies do not usually lend on a house with a lease of less than forty years to run; some even put the limit at sixty years.

But, thanks to the Leasehold Reform Act 1967, more and more leaseholds are capable of becoming freeholds. If you are interested in a leasehold house, find out whether the present owner has the right to buy the freehold. That right could be transferred to you. The house will be worth more with the right to buy than without it.

To benefit from the Act, the owner of the freehold must fulfil a number of requirements:

(1) The house must be your main residence. The majority of people consider one 'residence' all they can manage. But if for example you have a weekend cottage in the country and a house in town, the town house is the one to which the Act applies. Once you sell that and retire to your country cottage, the cottage becomes your main (or only) residence, and the Act applies to the cottage.

(2) You must have lived there for at least three years. This period can either be the three years just past, or three out of the last ten.

(3) During the material years you must have occupied the house either as owner or as a member of the owner's family. The owner's widow, for example, need not wait till she herself has owned the house for three years. She can use the Act three years after her husband bought the lease.

(4) The rateable value of the house on 23 March 1965 must

have been £200 or less in England or Wales (or £400 or less in London). If it is higher the Act does not apply.

(5) The ground rent must be less than two thirds of that rateable value. If it is higher, the Act does not apply.

(6) The lease must, originally, have been for more than twenty-one years. This does not mean that there must be a lot of it left when you buy.

Owners of houses to which all these points apply can usually – there are a few exceptions – insist on buying the freehold at a reasonable figure, or, if they prefer, get an extension of the lease for fifty years, at a higher rent.

How does this affect you, the house-hunter? Obviously you cannot insist on buying, or getting an extension of, the lease till you have lived in the house for three years. You may feel inclined to take a chance, move in and buy after that time. This is a little risky – the law may be changed, and you do not know how much the cost will be in three years – and should not be undertaken without advice from a solicitor or surveyor.

You could try a different solution: ask the seller of the house to apply to the landlord, and buy the house only when you know that the freehold can be bought on reasonable terms. You may have to come in on the seller's expenses, but your risk is reduced. Check with the lending institution of your choice that it is prepared to lend money on 'a leasehold with the right to purchase the freehold reversion'.

Buyers who are in the happy position of not needing a mortgage can sometimes pick up a lease of medium length at a much lower price than a comparable freehold house, but they should beware of buying during the last ten years or so, without having a very thorough survey of the house. At the end of the lease they have to return the house to the ground landlord. Not only do they have to return it, but it must be in the condition stipulated by the lease, and that lease commonly makes the lessee of the house responsible for keeping it well repaired and decorated. A house which has been up for some eighty or ninety years does not usually meet that standard, and at the end of the lease the lessee may have to pay compensation to the landlord. In short, at the beginning of a lease there is not much to choose between buying freehold or leasehold:

towards the end of a lease the same property may not be worth buying. The rent is low but the responsibilities are very high.

Part Possession

Buying a house with part possession, say of the ground floor, is quite different from buying a ground floor flat. Flats – old and new – are dealt with in Chapter 11.

Part possession of a house may give you the ground floor to live in, but will also give you a measure of responsibility for the rest of the house and its inhabitants. How much responsibility depends on what kind of agreement the other people in the house have with the present owner. Such an agreement can be written into a lease or tenancy agreement or can be by word of mouth. The Rent Acts may also influence the relationship between landlord and tenant.

If you are lucky, the upstairs tenants have a long lease with a full repairing liability. In other words they will have to contribute massively when the house needs repairs. Unfortunately, you are not likely to be offered that house with part possession. Far more probably, the owner of the house would offer you a flat on a long lease because, curiously enough, he or she could expect a better price that way.

No, the chances are that 'part possession' involves either a flat or some rooms for you, and a flat or further rooms occupied by tenants. It may be very nice to move into a house without being alone. Or again, it may not. If you do not get on with the tenants, you may nevertheless have to put up with them. You may not be able to raise their rent, you may not even be able to count on getting their accommodation when the present tenant dies and you outlive them. It is vital – if you don't want to risk nasty surprises later on – to get advice from your solicitor immediately.

Advantages: Price will be lower than for a flat of similar
              size
              Company in the house

Tenant provides you with an income

Some of the outgoings on the house can be set off before you pay tax on the rent you receive

Snags: Tenant's rent may be controlled by law at a low figure

Tenant may have the right to pass tenancy on to another member of the family

Tenant's habits may not agree with yours

You may have to pay for major repairs to tenant's accommodation

You are not likely to get a building society mortgage

You will have to pay income tax on your profit from letting.

Sitting Tenants

If you are the tenant of a house, or of a flat, the owner may be willing to sell the house to you at less than its normal price. The reason does not necessarily lie in the owner's great affection for you. Reasonably well-behaved tenants can, if they wish, continue to live in the place almost indefinitely. The owner, therefore, cannot sell the house as easily or for such a good price as the owner of a house without tenants.

If you are wise, you will talk to an estate agent or solicitor before you start negotiating with your landlord.

Local Authority Houses

After two years' occupation of council property, tenants can buy it if they wish. Before you do this, however, you would be wise to talk it over with your solicitors. For more details on the matter, see Chapter 12, p. 122.

Somebody Else Wants Your Chosen House

Make up your mind how badly you want the house. If you wish to buy it, do not delay. The sooner your solicitors make contact with the present owner's solicitors, the better your chances. Owners are usually impressed by the fact that a potential buyer is prepared to go to the length of visiting a solicitor. They accept it as a token of the buyer's seriousness. The solicitors will also be able to work out what they and you can do to speed up the buying process.

Various ways of trying to speed up the buying and selling of houses are being discussed. All need cooperation and none is foolproof. To give two examples: house-owners could make a local authority search as soon as they put their house on the market. This might save several weeks, because the search certificate might be available as soon as there is a purchaser (in the current system the purchaser makes the search). The house-owner of course has no guarantee that he will find a buyer within a reasonable period, before the search becomes out of date, nor can he be sure that the buyer will refund the search fee.

Also, there is much to be said for a mortgage certificate which allows a buyer to budget, but obviously such a certificate can only be valid for a relatively short time – the buyer's financial conditions may change.

Chapter 9

The Deposit

The word 'deposit' means different things to different people. Result: confusion. No one meaning is either right or wrong: this chapter explains how some of those concerned with deposits – house agents, building societies, house-buyers – think of them. Read this chapter to help you plan your house-buying, and do not conclude that because one person says you need a deposit of £x and another that you need only £y the second is necessarily offering you better terms. One estimate may well include something that another leaves out. What matters to you is: how much money of your own do you need to buy the house? Chapter 5, 'The Cost of Buying and Running a House', gave the answer.

The present chapter is intended to help you to know what the 'experts' are talking about, also whether and when to hand money over to them. The important thing about a deposit is that it should be paid to the right person at the right time.

Preliminary Deposit

When you first tell an estate agent that you want to buy the house which they have shown you, they will tactfully suggest that you should pay a deposit. Possibly the owners of the house, when you tell them the glad news that you want to buy, will themselves mention the deposit. Both the estate agent and the owners have the same thing in mind: there is many a slip between saying you will buy a house and actually buying it; how are they to know whether you mean business or whether you are giving voice to a pious hope? If you can be persuaded to put down money you are more likely to take this matter of house-buying seriously. They know, even if you do not at this point, that putting down a deposit does not bind you to go on with your purchase, but nevertheless . . .

It may be the other way round. You have fallen in love with a house and want to make sure of it. How better can you secure it than by putting down a deposit, reserving it to yourself?

Let us get this clear: both sides, buyer and seller, are bound only when they have exchanged contracts for the sale of the house (more about this on pp. 100, 138). Paying a deposit does not reserve the house to the eager buyer, nor does it bring certainty to the anxious seller.

This does not mean that you should never pay a preliminary deposit, but there are some guidelines which are worth following.

Very occasionally, a seller will reserve a house for a limited time on payment of a deposit. In such a case, check with a solicitor or some other reputable source that you are safe in paying.

Generally, sellers are more likely to put off other would-be buyers if they feel that you mean business. Some sellers are influenced by the fact that you have paid a deposit. Again, check before paying.

No one seriously expects you to pay more than a few hundred pounds at this stage; cautious buyers leave their cheque book at home and talk first to their solicitor. When the time comes, they pay the deposit through the solicitor, not direct to the seller.

If you pay a deposit to an estate agent, insist on a receipt and check its wording. Here is a typical receipt:

Received from Mr Peter Piper the sum of £   as preliminary deposit and in part payment of purchase money for the freehold property 14 Chestnut Avenue, Bursledon at the price of £   , subject to contract.
Received the above sum as stakeholders.

Two phrases are important. First, 'stakeholders': stakeholders are obliged to hold the deposit until completion of the sale; 'agents for the vendor' on the other hand are free to hand it over to the owner of the house. It is in your interest as buyer that the deposit money should remain where it is; if the sale is not completed you want your money back. The owner may need the deposit urgently and insist on it being paid to his solicitor as 'agent for the vendor'. The draft contract will make this clear. Your solicitors will warn you if the seller makes this condition. You are then in a dilemma: obviously, your deposit is safer if it cannot be touched by anyone. Against this, vendors may not be able to sell to you unless they can use your deposit. Perhaps they need it to pay a deposit on their new house; or perhaps the vendor is a builder who has borrowed money to build your new home and who wants to reduce his bank overdraft as quickly as possible. Ask your solicitors to find out the reason why the seller wants to use your deposit; you can then assess with them how much of a risk you are taking. I sometimes try a compromise: half the deposit to be at the vendor's disposal, the other half to be kept by the stakeholders until completion. Whatever you decide to do, at the early stage when an estate agent asks for a preliminary deposit, insist that they hold money you pay them 'as stakeholders'.

The words 'subject to contract' are even more important. They make it clear that you are not bound to buy the house till you exchange contracts. If for any reason, good or bad, you decide against signing a contract, you are entitled to claim your deposit back. This freedom is vital to you because at this stage you probably have no idea whether the house is soundly built (a survey will show), or whether you will be able to sell your own house in time, or whether you will be able to borrow enough money to buy. And it is always possible that one member of your family will take a dislike to the house, or that there are no suitable schools in the neighbourhood. It is true that, though you are not bound to go on, neither are the sellers. They are free to accept another offer at any time until contracts have been exchanged. You cannot reasonably expect to bind one side without binding the other. Fortunately, sellers are usually prepared to wait if they feel that you are serious about their house.

Important

Do not pay a deposit to the house-owner direct.
Get a receipt.

See that the words 'as stakeholder' and 'subject to contract' are included in the receipt.

Do not sign anything till your solicitor tells you to.

New Houses

Houses on new estates are often sold direct by the company developing the estate and are not offered through estate agents. Some estate developers refuse to deal with you until you have paid a deposit and signed a lengthy document. Paying a deposit in such a case usually means that the house will be reserved for you at its present price – find out for how long – but almost inevitably the document will contain conditions for which you may not have bargained. One document I saw told the buyer that his deposit would be used towards the purchase price if he exchanged contracts within six weeks. This sounds reasonable, but if he has read this book he will know the difficulty: once he signs on that particular dotted line he will have to buy that house or lose the deposit. In another case, the buyer was told nothing, not even shown building plans, until she had paid a non-returnable fee. Such a practice, though understandable from the developer's point of view, can add to house-buyers' expenses. They may have to risk the loss of this non-returnable deposit or decide not to buy on that estate at all. If the house looks good, they usually decide to pay the deposit.

Dealing with the Owner

It is not only on a housing estate that you may deal direct with the owner. Perhaps you found the house not through an agent but through a newspaper advertisement put in by the owner, or through personal recommendation. It is all right for you to tell the owner that you like the house, that you hope to buy it, and to agree on a price. But do no more. Ask the name of his or her solicitor, and, if a deposit is wanted, pay the solicitor through your own solicitor (see Chapter 8).

Warning
Do not pay the owner, or you may have difficulty in getting your deposit back if the sale does not go through.

10 Per Cent Deposit

A contract for the sale of a house almost invariably stipulates that on exchange of contracts the buyer should pay 10 per cent of the price; the remaining 90 per cent is paid on completion of the purchase. The exchange of contracts, however, means more than merely paying 10 per cent. The importance of exchanging contracts is that it marks the point of no return. Once you have exchanged contracts with the seller, you *must* buy the house. If you don't you lose the deposit and you may even have to pay compensation to the seller if the house is subsequently sold at a loss.

The 10 per cent deposit is not always paid at the moment when contracts are exchanged. You may not have heeded my earlier advice and have paid 10 per cent when you first decided on the house. Or you may have paid a preliminary deposit when you first decided to buy, and will bring the payment up to 10 per cent on exchange of contracts. Do not pay the owner direct. The best thing usually is to leave your money invested till it is needed. If it is in a savings account, or invested in securities, ask your solicitor to give you as much warning as possible so that you can get the deposit ready.

A further point worth consideration: when house prices and interest rates are high, you might try to persuade the owner to take a deposit of less than 10 per cent. You might reasonably argue that your deposit is meant to assure the owner that you will not break your contract, and that if he or she holds a few thousand pounds of your money they are sufficiently protected against your backing out. Or you might try to persuade the seller's solicitor to invest the deposit in a building society and to give you the interest. Either ploy is worth trying, but do not be disappointed if you are repulsed.

What if you have to sell your present house to raise the deposit on the new? Talk this over with your solicitors and with the manager of your bank. When you have a firm offer for your present house, the bank will probably lend you the 10 per cent without making too much difficulty (this is the famous 'bridging loan'). Of course, you will have to show that the sale of your present house will leave enough money over to repay the bank. The bank will probably also be willing to lend you money for the deposit for a few days while you sell securities or get money out of a deposit account. Obviously, you will save money if you can avoid borrowing.

If you are selling one house to buy another you could try to get the first deposit paid to your solicitors 'as agents for the vendor'. 'Agents for the vendor', unlike stakeholders, can use the money for the purposes of their client. It could therefore be used to provide the deposit on your new house and you would not have to borrow from your bank. Unfortunately, this convenient arrangement gives the buyer less security if the seller defaults; your buyer may insist on the deposit being held by stakeholders. But there is no harm in trying: more and more deposits are being used in this way when interest rates are high. Another way of coping if you cannot raise the deposit is by a deposit guarantee scheme.

Deposit Guarantee

Not surprisingly, there are insurance policies designed to reassure the present owners that they will not lose in the event of your not being able to complete your purchase. You may be able to buy such a policy for a single premium instead of paying a deposit. The premium is obviously less than a full deposit, but none of it counts towards the purchase price. Your solicitors can give you details; if your money is very well invested it may be worth paying a premium rather than cashing your investment a month before completion. Also, it is possible that the premium may cost less than a bridging loan from the bank. You cannot insist on such a policy: some owners feel more secure knowing that there is actual money on deposit.

95 Per Cent Mortgage

What if you have been promised a 95 per cent mortgage? You

have put by the remaining 5 per cent and enough to cover removal and legal fees, and worked out that you have just enough to cover all contingencies. Then all of a sudden you get a letter from your solicitors asking you for a 10 per cent deposit. Your first reaction may be that they have made a mistake and that they ought to have asked the building society for the money. But unfortunately they can't. The lender will not part with money before completion of the purchase. In the meantime contracts have to be exchanged or the sale will fall through.

There is usually a way out. You may be able to borrow part of the deposit, privately or from your bank, on the strength of the 95 per cent mortgage offer. Or you may be able to persuade the owner to accept a deposit of only 5 per cent. Provided you can satisfy his solicitor that you really have an offer of a 95 per cent mortgage and that there are no other snags, you may find that this is the easiest way out. If need be, you could offer a deposit guarantee for the other 5 per cent. Tell your solicitor on your very first visit that you are counting on a mortgage of more than 90 per cent and will not be able to raise a 10 per cent deposit. This will avoid last minute panic.

Size of Deposit

The most important thing from your point of view is not so much *when* you pay a deposit as *how much* you have to pay in all. Many house-buyers sensibly concentrate on working out how much they will have to find out of their own pocket, and look on that sum as 'the deposit'. Many building societies do likewise. When you apply for a mortgage, lenders always ask, 'How much are you going to contribute?' The answer in short is: the difference between the mortgage and the purchase price. This is explained in detail on p. 58 (capital contribution). But do not forget all the other figures of Chapter 5. The 'deposit', however you define it, is not all you need. Make sure, before you get too deeply involved in house-buying, that you have enough money to pay the deposit when contracts are exchanged; enough to buy the house and to pay all the

the attendant fees when the purchase is being completed; and that you can spare enough from your income to pay the outgoings once you have bought the house.

The final decision about the size of deposit lies with you. Once you have decided to buy, you have a choice. You could take the highest possible loan, with the result that your monthly mortgage payments will be high even if you do not use any of your savings. Or you could decide to put in as much of your capital as you can and to borrow as little as possible on mortgage. This will result in lower monthly mortgage repayments, but you will lose interest or dividends previously earned by your capital. Many buyers settle somewhere in between. There are some hints on these points on pp. 28–32.

Chapter 10

Surveyors

With your application for a mortgage you normally pay a fee, often called a 'survey fee', though not by responsible lenders, who are more likely to refer to an 'inspection fee' or a 'valuation fee'. This is more than a matter of words: before they commit themselves to lending money, lenders get a surveyor to inspect the house to make sure that it is worth lending on, i.e. that it is structurally sound and so forth.

Some lending organizations employ their own surveyors. Others instruct local surveyors to do the job. The thoroughness with which the inspection is made varies very much from one surveyor to another. Some inspect a house in great detail, others merely look at the outside, particularly if the house is in an area with which they are thoroughly familiar.

The surveyor makes a report to the lenders and may include in it comments on the state of repair of the house and suggestions for work which should be done. On the basis of this report the lenders either offer the amount for which you have asked or a lesser amount, or refuse your application. Or again they may say: you can have the loan but we shall hold back part of it till you have done certain repairs. They give you a list of repairs and usually set a time limit.

A typical example was that of a friend of Jones. He was offered a mortgage subject to a retention by the society till he had re-pointed the west wall. He was allowed six months to do the job. He took the smaller sum, bought the house, and immediately got in a builder. As soon as the pointing was complete, he told his solicitor. The surveyor came back to make sure that the work had been properly done and reported to the building society, which then handed over the balance less a small fee for their surveyor.

Many lenders lend up to about 80 per cent of their surveyor's valuation on a modern house, less on a house built before 1918. This figure can often be increased by an insurance policy, guaranteeing another 10 or 15 per cent, thus giving you a mortgage of up to 95 per cent. But you should understand that this is 95 per cent of the valuation, and not necessarily 95 per cent of the price you will have to pay for the house. You will be offered 95 per cent of the price only if in the surveyor's view the house is worth at least what you are paying for it. Mortgagees (lenders on mortgage), however, always play safe and point out that an offer of £x does not mean that in their view the house is worth that sum. On the other hand, a refusal by a lending institution to advance money on a particular house should make you think again. If they do not want to sink money into that house, do you really want to buy it? If they offer less than you have asked for, try to find out the reason. If the reason is connected with their surveyor's valuation, again ask yourself whether you are paying more than the house is worth.

The lenders' object in sending a surveyor is to make sure that next time the house is sold it is likely to fetch at least enough to repay the mortgage. Buyers want to know much more. Their concern is with the value, certainly, and they should if they have read the earlier chapters have a fair idea of values before they sign a contract. But it is even more important for them to know whether the house which they are about to buy has any defects not apparent on inspection, defects which may cost a lot to put right.

Some of the answers will be given, free of charge, by a firm of woodworm and dry rot specialists. There are many such firms. They give a report, an estimate of what it would cost to remedy the defect, and the promise of a guarantee for anything up to thirty years. It is worth remembering, though, that the firm does not guarantee to stay in business for thirty years. If you are looking for a mortgage on an old house, the lenders may well make it a condition that you get such a report. Look carefully at the estimate; it will explain what is included and what is not. A damp house drying out, for example, will often need a great deal done to its plasterwork. Such work is not always included in the estimate.

Houses built within the last few years may carry a National

House-Building Council certificate. This runs for a maximum of ten years and deals only with major defects. Neither an NHBC certificate nor a woodworm guarantee covers the full range of ills that can befall a house.

For this reason it is a good idea to have the house surveyed before you decide whether to buy. It would of course be simpler, and possibly cheaper, if the surveyor not only inspected the house for the lenders, but at the same time surveyed it for the purchaser. Indeed many people not surprisingly think that is what does happen. But they are wrong. Surveyors make a report to the lending organization, mainly on the value of the house. They do not make a survey of the structure, which is a much more detailed (and expensive) matter. If they value the house at a lower price than you are having to pay, they will tell the lenders. You will not necessarily be told how much lower, though some lending institutions are quite happy to show you a copy of the surveyor's report if you ask. If the surveyor makes a mistake, he is responsible to the mortgage company, which may decide never to employ him again. But you are still left with your mortgage debt.

Buyers should not deceive themselves. Without a full surveyor's report, made on their own instructions, they have not given themselves every chance of finding out about the house while there is time to pull back.

A budget which does not allow for repairs might be seriously thrown out by the sudden emergence of fractured drains, dry rot in the floor or settlement in the main walls. You are possibly even more exposed if you are buying a flat in a block which needs major repairs. However beautiful your own flat, you will either have to share in the cost of the repairs of the whole building or, if no one does them, the block and with it your flat may drop in value. It may take years for faults to show, but when they do you may have to spend a lot of money. It is possible for woodworm to be present for many years without being detected. It is also possible that the owner knows there is woodworm but does not tell you. Owners do not have to volunteer information about the defects of the house. All they need do is give a straight answer to your questions. Not being a surveyor, you will find it difficult to know what questions to ask. Even if you put the right questions, it is open to the owner to say: 'Come and look for yourself.'

In spite of the expense you would, therefore, be wise to employ a surveyor of your own. You may know one. If not, try to get a recommendation. You want a surveyor who is thorough and who takes responsibility for the job. You do not want to spend money on a report like one I once saw which excluded roof and floor boards and ended with a sentence to the effect that while every care had been taken no responsibility could be accepted for its contents. Many estate agents have at least one chartered surveyor in the partnership who can do the survey for you, but never employ a member of the firm that is selling you the house: their duty to the owner may conflict with their duty to you. It would also be better not to employ agents who are anxious to sell you a different house from the one they are being asked to survey. It is worth asking the mortgagees whether they will give you the name of the surveyor who looks at the house for them. He may be willing to do a full survey for you while he is at the house.* This is usually a little cheaper, and means one visit fewer for the harassed owner of the house. Not every surveyor who does valuation work also does full structural surveys. In some firms there are specialists for each job, emphasizing the fact that the two are by no means identical.

There is no set fee, so it is advisable to agree on one before telling the surveyors to go ahead. Also tell them exactly what you want done; their fee will depend on their professional qualifications, the size, age and accessibility of the house and on what work you expect them to do. Their ordinary fee may not include a test of the drains or of the electric wiring. If you want these checked, as you should in the case of an elderly house, tell them before they go. They may be able to do the job themselves or to arrange for someone else to do it.

Good surveyors will not only come back with a report of the state of repair obvious to the observant layman – cracks, broken tiles, etc. – but they will also cast an expert eye on the less obvious places and tell you whether the roof is sound, whether they suspect settlement, dry rot, wet rot, woodworm,

---

* Some building societies offer this option.

rising damp or any of the other ills which tend to befall houses. Do not be too shattered if your dreamhouse suffers from some of these. No house, it would seem, is completely free from defect. Furthermore, some go on happily in their defective state. The surveyors will tell you how serious the trouble is. If it can be put right, you can then ask a builder how much this would cost. You may well find that the owner is willing to pay part of the cost of remedying a defect; frequently a surveyor's report more than pays for itself. Of course, as well as a surveyor, you should get a specialist firm to check the house for wood-worm, dry rot, rising damp, etc.

Some chartered surveyors are willing to do a limited report for potential house-buyers for a much lower fee. Though useful, it leaves out a number of things a buyer is likely to want to know and is no real substitute for a complete survey.

Chapter 11

Buying a Flat or a New House

Flats

Not everyone takes kindly to the thought of living in a flat. Some people think of the dreadful experience of those whose flats have exploded, or collapsed, who were stuck in lifts, mugged, or marooned on the fifteenth floor. People on the continent do not necessarily love their flats, but have apparently come to terms with them. I often visit a friend in Rome whose balcony is a bower of roses, whose children have grown up without noticeable signs of deprivation, who never has to mow the lawn or to worry about muddy boots on the carpet. The flat is on the second floor; the common staircase not only absorbs mud and dust, but also provides a place where neighbours can meet.

The price of land in England is high: modern builders therefore tend to put as many dwellings on each plot as possible. More and more flats are being built, particularly in large cities. More and more people are, therefore, now thinking about buying a flat, particularly for their first home. Flats fall, roughly, into three groups: conversions, older purpose-built flats and modern flats.

Conversions

A large family house, often Victorian – intended for a large Victorian family with its complement of many children, maiden aunts and servants – is cut up into several flats. In a building of three or four floors this may result in three, four, six or even eight spacious and attractive self-contained units, each with its own access, kitchen, bathroom, etc. However, not every conversion is done with an eye to beauty and suitability. It could be a neglected house, divided into separate units by sheets of hardboard, with downpipes sprouting under the windows.

A converted flat can sometimes be found in a neighbourhood where there are few flats; it may have interesting proportions, and it may cost less than a purpose-built flat.

More and more first-time buyers look for conversions. They value the extra space, the funny corners, the low price. There are snags through: they may end up in draughty, high-ceilinged rooms, with a lot of noise from next door and nowhere to park the car. Some companies are disinclined to lend on conversions.

Purpose-built Flats (originally intended for letting)

Such flats were often built in big cities in the years before 1939. By modern standards they tend to be spacious, are usually well constructed and in substantial buildings. Being built for letting, there is sometimes a supply of hot water, or central heating, from one central source. There may even be a communal restaurant, a lift, or a porter. Such flats are often modernized by the owner of the building as tenants move out, and then offered for sale. They are often less expensive than more recently built flats, and they are frequently far more solid. Against this, communal services may be more expensive than those you provide yourself: are you not more careful with hot water for which you receive a quarterly bill than with water from a boiler you have never seen?

Modern Flats (those built since about 1960)

Because of the high price of land and because the Rent Acts make being a landlord hazardous and unprofitable, almost all privately built flats are put up with a view to sale. Each flat is usually provided with its own front door as well as its own means of heating.

The advantages of such a flat are usually most obvious to young couples, though older couples whose children have grown up and moved away may find them equally useful. The majority of these flats have one or two bedrooms and one living room. The kitchen is usually equipped with built-in cupboards. Sometimes there are also built-in wardrobes, wood-block flooring or other luxuries. There is no difficulty about getting a maximum mortgage. Very little furniture is needed to make a flat into a home. The price both of buying and of maintaining a modern flat is probably lower than that of a house.

The snags? The rooms in such flats tend to be small, with little space for large pieces of furniture or for the accumulated junk of a happy family. The flat may or may not provide a reasonable standard of sound-proofing; you live at close quarters with your neighbours and cannot afford to fall out with them. In some London suburbs so many flats are being built that it may become more difficult to sell them. The cost of maintenance cannot be controlled by you (more about this later in this chapter), whereas in your own house you can decide not to paint this year because of unexpected roof repairs.

Very Important

Make sure the lease of the flat you intend to buy has a good number of years left. A new or newly converted flat will probably offer a lease of at least ninety years. You may think thirty or forty quite long enough for your needs, but it is not: you will be putting down several thousand pounds to buy that lease and you will probably want to sell it again. A lease with under forty-five or fifty years to run will be hard to sell. Nor is anyone likely to grant a mortgage on it. The chief worry of every building society, or of any lender for that matter, is that the building must keep its value at least until the mortgage is repaid. To be on the safe side, try for a flat where the lease will go on for a minimum of another seventy years.

Let us follow Jack String on his hunt for a flat. Life in a flat comes naturally to him: his mother has lived in one since she was widowed many years ago. Jack remembers the joy of racing up to the sixth floor while a more sedate adult made his ponderous way up by lift. His mother's flat is on the top floor of a block of flats built in about 1925. The flat used to have a

view over the river, and now has a view over chimneys and
TV aerials. She chose a top floor because she loves Italian
opera, which she plays loudly at all hours. The block of flats,
being somewhat old-fashioned, has only two flats on each
floor, divided by a stairwell. Very little sound, therefore, travels
from her flat to her neighbours'. There is a resident porter who
admits callers only after checking with the owner of the flat,
and there has never been a burglary. He also operates the lift
and, if asked nicely, unstops the sink and mends fuses for
Jack's mother.

Jack is in the pleasant stage between bachelordom and
marriage, and his girlfriend will probably come to share the
flat; they have little furniture between them. They have looked
at a flat rather like his mother's but decided against it because
the central-heating system serving the block was some forty
years old and likely to need replacing before long. Jack did not
want to be saddled with a major expense of this kind. Nor can
he easily afford the porter's wages or the upkeep of the thick
carpets on the stairs.

Jack works in the West End of London. He has come to the
view that whereas the choice in his favourite area, Kensington,
is very restricted at a price he can afford, there seem to be
very many flats to be had further out. After receiving a list of
some fifty flats from one agent and inspecting several of these,
he decides to make a detailed list of his requirements:

Must have	*Would like*
Price below £x thousand	Price about £x thousand
Near public transport	Separate W C
Three rooms	Garden
Full central heating	Fitted carpets
	Double glazing
	East/west aspect
	Balcony

Jack's girlfriend has ideas of her own. She does not make a
list but makes a mental note to look out for a flat with a
balcony and with space for a pushbike or a pram either in the
flat or elsewhere in the building.

Eventually Jack visits Dragon Court. On either side of the
entrance of a stark modern building there are two heraldic

beasts justifying the name of the Court. The entrance hall is carpeted; he cannot hear himself walk. The staircase is covered in vinyl which is slightly noisy but means that the stairs will not need recarpeting every few years. The sound of shuffling footsteps is a good deal less obtrusive than on the concrete stairs Jack has climbed in some of the other blocks he looked at. Jack is impressed. The flat itself has a small lobby with doors to all rooms, another good point in his eyes. In several other flats one had to go through the lounge to reach the bathroom and bedrooms. This might suit a young family, but does not allow for grown-ups who want to get in and out without disturbing one another.

There is full central-heating – another plus point: some flats have central heating in only two rooms; in others the water has to be heated separately by gas or electricity. Jack likes a warm bathroom and plenty of hot water at reasonable cost. Bathroom and WC are combined; indeed Jack has seen no modern flat at a price he could contemplate which afforded the luxury of a separate lavatory.

The bedrooms face east, the lounge west, ideal for a sun-worshipper who is out during the day: he would wake up to sunlight and be home again to enjoy the evening sun. The view from the living room is on to a paved area, interrupted by standard roses and ornamental trees – pleasant to look at and simple to maintain.

The owner tells Jack that he intends to leave behind the fitted carpets in two rooms. Jack makes a note to check with his solicitor – he has decided that this is the flat for him – whether the lease requires him to carpet the flat throughout.

In some of the very new flats which Jack has seen the rooms were so tiny that they would hardly hold his small store of furniture. This flat is some fifteen years old and not quite so tightly planned. Jack also remembers what a surveyor friend has told him: a building needs a few years to show whether it is going to have problems. After ten or twelve years one can tell whether cracks are serious or not.

Next day Jack telephones the estate agent and makes an offer, a little below the asking price. After looking at the list of flats it seems to Jack that he has a reasonable chance of getting this reduction. The agent telephones back within the hour: the owner will take a reduction half-way between his price and Jack's offer. Jack accepts gracefully and tells the agent to go ahead. He gives him the name and address of his own solicitors. Jack then rings his solicitors and tells them of the intended purchase. He also makes an appointment with them a fortnight ahead. By then the solicitors ought to have received a copy of the lease from the owner's solicitors, and should be able to tell Jack about its good and bad points.

Next, Jack goes to the building society with whom he wisely put his savings some years earlier. The manager of the building society has already told Jack that he can have the money he needs, provided the flat passes muster. When Jack visits his solicitors they go through the lease together. Practically all flats in England (not so in Scotland) are offered for sale on long leases (leasehold). The general rule that freehold has the edge on leasehold does not apply to flats or maisonettes. There are reasons, buried in legal history, which make it difficult for one freehold-owner to force another to look after his or her flat. And if the people above and below you will not look after the paintwork of their flats, your own flat will probably lose value. Worse still, if the gutter on the top floor is allowed to leak, the people on all floors below may suffer from damp walls. Other things being equal, try to buy a flat leasehold. In an old flat it can nevertheless happen that no one is responsible for upkeep of the building. Modern flats are usually well organized in this respect.

Often the land and those parts of the building not forming part of any flat (the common parts) are either left in the hands of the builder, or sold to a management company in which each flat-owner has a share. From the flat-owner's point of view, a management company is probably the most labour-saving way of having the block well maintained. The company works on a business footing and charges for the work it does. The charges are fairly strictly controlled by law. Before the company orders expensive work, the flat-owners must be consulted and several estimates obtained. The flat-owners themselves sometimes feel that they could arrange the work more cheaply. Residents who are prepared to spend time on this can ask different firms for estimates, do some of the work themselves and get to know one another as well as save money. In my experience flat-owners can be rallied when there is a crisis (e.g. a very large bill), but they are unlikely to take a continued interest in running a block.

At Dragon Court the running of the block is in the hands of a firm of estate agents. Jack was concerned that this might be very expensive, but is reassured when the present owner tells him that he has had to pay only a few pounds a week, including insurance of the flat.

Dragon Court follows a fairly common pattern. The block of flats stands back from the road; there is a separate block of garages, and a place where all the dustbins are kept. All flats are reached through the same front door, entrance hall and staircase. An answerphone at the front door communicates with all flats.

When the flats were built, the builder granted a 99-year lease for each flat. Each lease contains a clause saying that there is a yearly rent of £20 for each of the first 30 years, after which the rent goes up to £50 a year. That rent (the 'ground rent') is paid by the owner of the flat to the owner of the land. His lease gives the flat-owner the right to use the communal parts he needs: a right to walk from the street to his own front door, from his flat to the dustbin and to the garden, a right to use the garden and a right to drive his car to his garage.

He also gets the right to enter an adjoining flat in an emergency, and similarly he must allow his neighbours to come into his flat if, for instance, there is a gas leak, or water coming through the ceiling. He will have to keep his flat in good repair – the lease says what bits are his and what bits will be done communally. At Dragon Court each flat-owner looks after the interior and the landowner looks after the outside. The lease obliges each flat-owner to contribute to the cost of the communal work, and to the cost of insuring the block against fire, etc. The landowner in his turn promises to repair and insure the building and to look after the common parts.

During the fortnight before he went to see his solicitors, Jack thought of a number of points. He now tries to get them clarified:

(1) Will he need carpets throughout the flat? If everyone has to carpet throughout, the flats will be quiet but the expense considerable.

(2) Will he have to pay stamp duty on the rent? No, because this is not a new lease. When the lease was granted to the first flat-owner, it was stamped. The stamped lease will form part of Jack's title deeds. Jack himself is liable for stamp duty only on the price he pays for the flat. The agreed price, £30,100, includes fitted carpets. Jack pays for these separately and saves. Houses and flats attract stamp duty, carpets don't. By buying the latter separately, it may be possible to pay less stamp duty, or none at all. A flat bought for £30,100 including £500 worth of carpets attracts stamp duty at 1 per cent, i.e. £301. However, there is no stamp duty on a flat bought for £29,600 (being below the £30,000 threshold for stamp duty), nor on carpets, however expensive. Jack can therefore save £301 by telling his solicitor that he is buying the owner's carpets.

(3) Does he repair the outside of his flat? No, but he has to pay a proportion of the cost of maintaining Dragon Court in good order. This point is particularly important for the buyer of a top floor flat. If he is solely responsible for his flat (including the roof) he must have the roof carefully surveyed: roof repairs are very expensive.

(4) Are there any major outstanding repairs? It would be wise to get a survey done. Show the surveyor a copy of the lease.

(5) How easy is access to all parts of the building which may need repair or maintenance? If the window cleaner needs a cradle he will charge more than if he can reach all windows with ease. If the back of the house can be reached only over the roof or through your flat, repairs could be both expensive and inconvenient. (Victorian conversions and flats over shops are particularly apt to have this problem.)

A modern flat is as popular with most lenders as a modern house. You will be able to borrow the same high percentage on either. Just occasionally one society's rules work against a particular type of lease. You are unlikely to change the provisions of the lease, so go to another source of money. If you are buying a flat in a brand-new development, the developer may have made arrangements with a particular firm. Ask about this – you are not obliged to use that firm but it may save time and trouble to try them first of all.

New Houses

Similar rules apply to new houses – suppliers of mortgages are glad to lend. Provided your income is large enough for the mortgage, you can probably borrow 90 to 95 per cent of their valuation.

If the house is completely built when you decide to buy, no special precautions are necessary, except to ask whether it carries a National House-Building Council certificate. Buying a house without NHBC insurance could lead to a problem when reselling, at least within the ten years' protection provided by the certificate.

It helps to buy on an estate where you can see at least one completed show house. Try to disregard its tasteful furnishing and find out what will come with your house and what has to be paid for separately. In times of sluggish sales there may be extras included in the price to induce you to buy. A very helpful incentive of this sort is aid with the mortgage in case of redundancy.

When there are more buyers than houses, every house on an estate may well be sold before the first one has been built. At such times you may see some rather elegant pictures and be told that the house will have a modern shower suite. Many new houses have one touch of luxury and very nice it is too, but do not be dazzled by the glamour of a fitted kitchen; what you really need is a solidly built house whose walls and roof will stand up to time. If the building gives little trouble, you will be able to afford a beautiful interior; you will, on the other hand, get little comfort when the wind blows through cracks in the walls of your sun room with jacuzzi.

You might well have to buy before your house is actually ready. Make sure you know precisely *what* you are buying – which plot will be yours, where will your garden be, which way will various rooms be facing, is there a garage?

You will probably be fighting a losing battle if you try to get a firm completion date from a builder. Resign yourself to the fact that it will probably be later than the first optimistic date you were given. Stick out, though, for the right to four weeks notice before you have to produce the purchase money. This is

particularly important if you are selling your present house to
buy a new one.

Also, find out whether the builder can increase the price
quoted to you. Your solicitor can advise on whether there is
any hope of preventing this. Check on how the house will be
heated, whether central heating extends to all rooms and
whether there is double glazing. Compare the room measurements given with the size and proportion of actual rooms. The
building specification itself is something on which you would
do well to get a surveyor's opinion. Be very suspicious of a
builder who refuses to disclose plans and specifications before
you have signed a binding contract.

Again, make sure the house will have an NHBC insurance
cover. It is given only to builders who agree to build to the
standards laid down by the National House-Building Council.
The Council inspects the house periodically during construction. The builder guarantees that the house is constructed
according to the Council's standards (or to the conditions laid
down in the building contract where these are higher) and
that it will be built in a workmanlike manner and be fit for
human habitation.

The builder agrees to make good any defects appearing
within two years because of a breach of these standards –
other than cracks, etc. caused during the drying-out process.
Central heating is covered for one year only.

If the builder should go out of business during the guarantee
period, the Council steps into his place.

For a further eight years the Council itself undertakes to
make good major defects, such as a collapsing roof, or severe
damage caused by subsidence. The maximum insurance cover
goes up each year in step with inflation.

It is a useful guarantee, and the majority of reputable builders
are content to give it. Even if you yourself would be prepared to
do without, you should spare a thought for the future when
you may want to sell the house. Building societies are becoming increasingly reluctant to lend money on houses without
the NHBC insurance: more about this in the booklet *Your New
House*, prepared by the National House-Building Council.

Stage Payments

All the houses so far mentioned have to be paid for in the same way: 10 per cent on exchange of contracts and the balance on completion.

Some new houses, particularly those put up by small firms, are paid for in a different way: by stage payments. The contract provides for a down payment and for further instalments when the building is up to the first floor, up to roof level, ready for plastering, etc. As each stage is reached, the builder collects an instalment. Lenders can usually be persuaded to provide money as each stage is reached, though not until their surveyors have had a look at the construction and declared themselves satisfied. A small fee is charged for each inspection. Also, each instalment bears interest as soon as it is handed over. Stage payments benefit the builder rather more than the house-buyer, who has to make mortgage payments *before* there is a house to move to. Some builders, recognizing the buyer's problem, offer a rented house while the new one is being built. This makes it possible to sell the old home, invest the money and pay it out to the builder as each stage is reached.

Buying a Plot

You may be in luck if you are offered a plot of land. Make sure that it has planning permission for the kind of building you would like to put on it. Outline permission for one private house is likely to allow just that; don't count on putting up two and a chicken farm.

Ready-made designs for houses can be bought for less than an architect's fee; they do, however, have a way of not fitting your plot. You need imagination as well as a reliable builder.

If the plot is in the country, do not forget the dull details – how far must electricity be brought, how will the property be drained, has the plot access to a road, etc.?

You may well get a much better, though certainly a more expensive, house if you have it specially designed for your plot and your needs.

Chapter 12

Other Possibilities

Buying an Old House

Perhaps you are thinking of buying an old house because of its mellowness, its beautiful proportions, its Adam fireplace. A house of that kind needs a constant supply of money and love, and it is as well to remember that when you run out of one or both you cannot jettison your erstwhile love without finding a successor. You will probably take the advice of a surveyor or an architect before deciding on the purchase.

At the other end of the financial scale, you may well be thinking of an old house, not because it is beautiful but because it costs less than a modern one. 'Old' in this context is not so much a matter of years as of lack of amenities. From time to time there are houses on the market without such aids to gracious living as a bathroom or a WC. They are well worth considering, provided they are structurally sound – and provided you can get a mortgage. The absence of modern amenities can be an advantage, because you will almost certainly be able to claim a grant from the local authority to help provide them. How much you can hope to get depends on where you live, what improvements you want to make and how hard up the local authority is. You are entitled to some grants as of right, others are given at the discretion of the local authority. Get a copy of the booklet *Your Guide to House Renovation Grants* from your local council and talk to them before you commit yourself.

Homesteading

In some areas where there are many elderly houses in need of restoration, local authorities buy them up and resell them to first-time buyers at reasonably favourable prices. If you are good at DIY, find out whether your council runs the Homesteading Scheme and get particulars from them.

The houses are sold subject to a condition that you carry out specified repairs. The usual grants are available and the council keeps a close eye on your progress, setting a time limit for completing work. The advantage is that you don't have to start making mortgage payments until the limit is reached.

Buying a Thatched Cottage

A thatched cottage, if well looked after, should be acceptable to most providers of mortgages. Insurance rates will be higher than for a tiled or slated roof: the Country Gentlemen's Association may be able to make recommendations.

Buying by Auction

The 'Property for Sale' columns in newspapers, and advertisements in London underground stations, often offer houses for sale by auction. As a general rule these are either houses for investment, sold with a 'sitting tenant', or one-off houses for which it is not easy to fix a market price. However, at a time when there are more sellers than buyers, even run-of-the-mill houses might be offered at auction. Bear in mind that many houses advertised for sale by auction are sold privately.

Let us assume you are attracted to a house offered by auction. First see the agent and try to find out what sort of price the owner expects, or hopes for. If the agent won't tell you, make a tentative offer and see whether the owner is prepared to sell before auction at your figure. If not, and you are still keen on the house, you must inevitably spend money before you know whether you are going to be successful at the auction, because the acceptance of your bid means that you have to sign a binding contract immediately after the auction. By that time, therefore, you must be sure that you will be able to raise the money, are satisfied about the soundness of its construction, and have explored its future with the local authority. Get advice on this from a solicitor well before the auction.

Buying by Tender

Occasionally a house is bought in this manner: you are asked to make an offer. If this is accepted you must buy. Make sure you have made all the inquiries recommended for auction sale *and* have taken advice on what is a reasonable price. Not a method to be advised.

Right to Buy

Council tenants of at least two years' standing can buy their houses or flats if they wish. The price is at least 32 per cent less than market value: the longer you have been a tenant the greater your discount. After 30 years, tenants are entitled to a 60 per cent discount. The maximum discount, however, is £35,000. For flats the discount begins at 44 per cent after two years and can go up to 70 per cent, or £35,000.

If you are interested in buying and think that you qualify, fill in an application form. The council will give you a price and may also make a mortgage offer. Councils and building societies are often happy to lend 100 per cent of the reduced price you are asked to pay. If you resell within three years you have to repay part of the discount.

Before you decide to buy, consider:
Is the house/flat in reasonable repair?
If not, how much will it cost to put it into an acceptable state? Can you increase your mortgage to pay for repairs or improvements?

How does your rent compare with the mortgage, rates (or community charge) and heating you will have to pay after you have bought?

Allowing for this extra expense, is it still a bargain?

Buying from Executors

It may well be of no interest or significance that a house is being sold by executors. When you buy a house through an advertisement or an estate agent you may not even be told that it is the late owner's executor who is selling. Some executors fear the knowledge of a recent death in a house may detract from its saleability.

It does not follow that executors will sell more cheaply than other owners. Occasionally, however, you can pick up a house, perhaps a little old-fashioned, not too recently painted or papered, at a lower price, simply because the executor lives a long way off and does not want the responsibility of maintenance. Or, the proceeds of sale may have to be shared by several people: a reduction, sizeable to you, may only mean a couple of hundred pounds less for each of them. There are several other reasons why an executor's sale may mean a bargain. Don't rely on this, but keep your eyes open for the possibility.

Co-ownership Housing Associations

If you have spent the past few years sharing a flat, your main idea in buying a house may well be to gain a little privacy. You may not warm to the idea of further communal effort. On the other hand, you will have learnt that by pooling your resources with others, you live much better than you could have done on your own.

Most housing associations exist to make rented homes available, but there are possibilities for those who want to own. A recent development is the *shared ownership* scheme.

Co-ownership does not mean that you share your house; it means that the association owns a development, and you own shares in the association together with the right to occupy a particular property. You do not own that particular house or flat. This may not matter to you while you live there. Your 'rent' is likely to be lower than normal *and* it qualifies for mortgage interest relief.

What happens when you wish to leave? Not being an 'owner' you cannot sell your house, or your lease. But you can sell your share in the association. The rules of the association will lay down how much you can expect. Very roughly, this will be what you have put in, plus, if you have lived there for a number of years, a share in the increased value of the association property, less any outstanding liabilities. Obviously, if you leave after a short time you will get little or nothing, but the same may well be true of a house which you bought on mortgage. In the long run your profit on leaving tends to be lower than on a privately owned house.

Self-Building

An excellent alternative to buying a house for those with (1) skills useful to housebuilding (for example, architect, surveyor, bricklayer, plasterer) and (2) perseverance. A group of people combine to build a number of houses, all members of the group giving their services free. The cost of materials is provided by mortgage with perhaps some contribution from members. As each house is completed it is made available to one of the members on loan, without protection from the Rent Acts. When all houses are finished each member can buy a house at a price which covers only the land, the building expenses and the mortgage. The members then each get a mortgage of their own and become independent.

Shared Ownership

Some housing associations build blocks of flats for this purpose. Instead of buying the whole flat you buy a share in that flat and you rent the remainder. Although your purchase deed will put it in percentage terms, you buy – as it were – the living room and you pay rent for the rest. When you can afford some more, you buy the kitchen and pay rent only on the bedroom and bathroom, and so on, until you have either bought the whole flat or you want to sell.

This scheme may help you to find a roof over your head at a time when you cannot really afford to buy, but it is not a cheap method of buying. You buy your first slice today at today's value; by the time you buy your next slice, the value of the flat (and therefore the price of that slice) will have gone up. Indeed, not all housing associations allow you to build up your share. Instead you may have to buy 50 or 75 per cent and rent the rest. Also, there may be restrictions on who you can sell to when you want to move out.

Advice on these last three schemes is obtainable from the Housing Corporation, Maple House, 149 Tottenham Court Road, London W1. To summarize:

Co-ownership:
  Advantages: Low capital contribution, favourable mortgage terms
       Snags: Difficult to find
              Even more difficult to form a new association
              Mortgage funds not always available
              Takes a long time.

Self-build:
The same advantages and disadvantages, plus
  Advantages: Standard of workmanship will probably be very high
              Low cost
        Snag: Special skills required.

Shared ownership:
  Advantage: You may be able to buy in stages as your means allow

Snags: You may not find a housing association with shared ownership flats in the area you want

Later slices are likely to cost more than the first one

You get tax relief only on your mortgage payment, not on your rent.

Part 3

Why It Takes So Long

Chapter 13

Solicitors' Work Before Contract

It is vital, if you want to buy a house as quickly as possible, to go to a solicitor as soon as you and the owner have agreed on a price and before you have committed yourself. Nevertheless, quite often solicitors know nothing of their client's intention to buy a house until they get a letter from an estate agent, like the following:

Dear Sir,

re: 14 Chestnut Avenue, Bursledon

Acting on the instructions of Mr George Smith, we have sold the above property to Mr Peter Piper for £   . We understand that you act for Mr Piper. The vendor's solicitors are Messrs Blower & Co. of 8 High Street, Southampton, whom we have asked to send you a draft contract.

In the meantime, Mr Piper has paid us a preliminary deposit of £100. We enclose a copy of our receipt.

Yours faithfully,

Although agents often say they 'have sold' a house, in fact they have not at this stage. What they mean is that they are hoping to sell. The phrase, though often used by estate agents, does not bind you to go on with the purchase. Not, that is, unless you have disregarded the advice given in earlier chapters. Provided you have written no imprudent letters and signed no papers, you are not at this stage bound to buy. Equally, George Smith can change his mind about selling.

If the solicitors have not heard from Peter Piper before, they write to him now for confirmation. Peter might reply:

Dear Ms Stokes,

Thank you for your letter. Yes, I am hoping to buy 14 Chestnut Avenue, Bursledon. The price is £   . I have applied for a

mortgage of £   . I shall write to you again as soon as I know
whether I can get enough money.

Yours sincerely,

Peter Piper

This tells the solicitors that Peter Piper is uncertain whether
he will get his mortgage and does not want to incur solicitors'
fees till he knows.

However, if he is in a hurry or is willing to risk a few
pounds' extra expense, Peter will write a slightly different
letter:

Dear Ms Stokes,

   Thank you for your letter. Yes, I am hoping to buy 14 Chestnut
Avenue, Bursledon. The price is £   . I have paid the agents
£100 and have applied to the   Building Society, from whom
you should be hearing shortly. Please in the meantime do what you
can to speed up the purchase. I would like to move in seven weeks'
time if possible.

Yours sincerely,

Peter Piper

This gives the solicitors the green light; it also tells them that
everything will have to go according to programme, or seven
weeks will not be long enough to see the purchase through.

Ms Stokes writes to the vendor's solicitors, Blower & Co.,
and asks for a draft contract. She may get it by return of post,
or may have to wait while the owner's solicitors track down
the title deeds. To draft a contract a solicitor has to know what
is in the title deeds. Prudent house-owners tell their solicitor as
soon as they decide to sell the house. By the time they have
found a buyer the solicitor will have either the deeds or a copy.
Sometimes this is quite simple: some owners keep the deeds at
home, some in their bank, and can send them to their solicitor.
But when there is a mortgage on the house, there may be
delay. The title deeds are with the lender – the bank, building
society or insurance company. Some lending organizations
keep all deeds at their head office, others at different branches.

In the meantime, the buyer's solicitors will try to see their
client and get all the information they need to do the job. Here is
a list of questions to which sooner or later your solicitor will
need the answers. It helps to have them ready for your first visit:

your full name and present address – for the purchase deed;
your occupation;
address of the new house;
present owner's name;
price;
freehold or leasehold;

whether you are buying through agents. If so, their name and address;

whether you have paid a deposit and how much;

whether you need a mortgage and whether you have already applied for one (see below);

when you would like to move (see over);

whether you have to sell a house before you can buy this one;

whether you are buying any furniture with the house;

any fixtures;

whether you are buying in your sole name or with somebody else (see over);

Most important: how definite are you about this house? When do you want the solicitors to start seriously on the legal work? As soon as you give your solicitors the go-ahead, they will make local authority searches and send out inquiries before contract (see pp. 134–7).

Mortgage

If you have not yet applied for a mortgage your solicitors will be able to advise you. If the bulk of the purchase money is to be raised on mortgage, they will probably suggest that you visit one or two possible sources of money before you go further with your plans. Don't spend more on solicitors' fees till you know you can get a mortgage which is big enough to allow you to buy the house of your choice. What you *can* do is ask your solicitors to get a draft contract from the owner's solicitor. Once that has been sent out you will almost certainly be warned before the owner deals seriously with any other buyer. This is probably the nearest you can get to an assurance that the house will not be sold to anyone else.

Moving Date

Remember that the date of the contract is not the date you move house. It is probably too early to fix a moving date, though it is convenient to plan about two months ahead – four weeks till contracts are signed, another four before moving. Do not make rigid plans, because you cannot rely on a date till you have exchanged contracts. There is a lot to do before you reach that stage. In particular, do not buy curtains or anything which might not fit equally well into another house should this deal fall through.

If this is the first house you are buying you may have to give your present landlord at least four weeks' notice. Tell your solicitors about this and they will arrange for you to know a month before you move. As soon as contracts are exchanged get in touch with removal firms, particularly if your move is planned for a weekend, a quarter day or near the end of the month – times at which they get most heavily booked.

The usual thing is to pay over your purchase money for the key of the house. Solicitors and agents talk of the 'completion date' – the day on which your purchase is finally tied up. Some owners allow the buyer to move in before completion, charging him rent in the meantime, but most prefer a straight exchange of money against key.

One Name or Joint Names?

Many couples feel that both husband and wife work to keep the house going and that they want to share in the ownership, so they buy the house in joint names.

A wife, particularly if she puts money into a house for the family, will probably feel more secure if her name is on the title deeds. She can be protected by law even if it is not, but anyone whose marriage is somewhat shaky would do well to talk to a solicitor at this stage.

Normally, when husband and wife buy in joint names, they do this with the idea that when one of them dies the other will automatically have the house. In law this is buying as 'joint tenants'. Some couples (or other joint buyers) prefer an arrangement whereby each can leave his/her share in the house to somebody else. This is buying as 'tenants in common', and is what the couple in the Land Certificate on pp. 144–6 have done. The reason might be that a third party, perhaps Mary Bennett's parents, has lent one of them money informally and the borrower wants to repay it on sale or death; or there could be tax reasons – a couple may well save Inheritance Tax by giving a share in the house to their children rather than to each other; or one of them may have children from an earlier marriage and wish them to have a share in the house. Another advantage of buying as tenants in common is that joint owners can own the house in unequal shares. If, for example, Jack and Libby had decided to buy a house together, her contribution would have been bigger than his, because she came out of her divorce with a capital sum. They might have decided that she should own a bigger share in the house.

Selling One House and Buying Another

When you sell one house and buy another you will probably need the money from your present house to pay for the new one. Your buyer won't hand over the money except against your key, and you can't give up your old house except to move into the new. So both sales have to be completed on the same day. This can be a matter of considerable anxiety to you *and* to your solicitor: if anyone along the line is not ready in time, the whole transaction totters. When finance is fairly easy, a bank will often lend money for the new house pending the sale of the old – this is called a bridging loan.

Bridging Loan

Banks prefer to lend money for a short and definite period: ideally they want to be assured that you have a firm buyer for your old house and have exchanged contracts with him. This usually has to be confirmed by your solicitor direct to the bank.

A word of warning: bank loans are expensive. You have to pay interest, and in addition usually a fee for the work involved. Also, whenever government policy is against lending money, bridging loans are early victims. The solicitor can advise you on whether you are likely to have difficulty with your moving date, and what chance you have of a bridging loan. See your bank manager if you are likely to need a loan.

Local Authority Searches

Whenever they are concerned with buying a house, solicitors send a great number of questions to the local authority. They do not have a free hand in asking; they cannot ask how much the mayor paid for his own house, or whether the road is noisy. Questions have to be selected from about sixty agreed between the local authorities and the Law Society. The solicitors pay a fee, also agreed.

What happens when the questions reach the local authority? In a typical London borough all questions go to the Land Charges Department, which then collects the answers from other departments. For example, the Public Health Department will be asked about smoke control or drainage, and the Borough Engineer whether the road is maintained at public expense. Eventually the questionnaire is returned to the solicitors with answers to all questions. How long it takes for a local authority to provide them varies considerably. Some local authorities send the answers back within a week, others take much longer. Where a house lies in the area of an authority that takes a long time, a solicitor may advise that the inquiries should be put in even before you are quite sure that you will go through with the buying of the house. There is talk of local authorities being forced by law to reply in fourteen days, but there is no such law in force at the moment. There is also talk of the information being made available, instantly, on computer. This project is not far beyond the pipedream stage. Indeed it is often necessary to make personal searches to avoid losing a house. In the last few years a number of firms have grown up specializing in visiting local authorities to make these searches. Many of these firms take out insurance to protect house-buyers against errors. If they were to miss something vital you would be able to sue them for compensation. A personal search through a firm of this kind does inevitably add to the cost of buying.

The solicitors go through the answers and tell the buyer of any that may particularly affect him. For example, if the council plans to take over the private road outside the house, the owner of each house affected would have to contribute to the expense of making up the road. This could in effect add to the price of the house. If the council has got to the stage of knowing how much it will charge each frontager, it may be possible to get this contribution from the present owner. If the plan is at an early stage, the council may not know how much the work will cost. The buyer's solicitors will at least be able to warn their client.

Then there is smoke control. If a Smoke Control Order is to come into force in the near future, the house-owner will get a contribution from the local authority to convert open fires. Buyers can be warned not to lay in large supplies of fuel which they will not be able to use.

It is vital for every newly built house to fit in with the plans approved by the local authority. A buyer has to be sure, for example, that the house is not nearer the road than the authorized building line – it may have to be torn down if it offends. Or, again, there may be plans for road widening which might affect either house or garden. Or the drains, if private, might be taken over by the local authority – at the owner's expense. This can be required if there is a public sewer within 100 yards of the house. The search form will show whether there is.

As solicitors' questions have to follow a set formula, it is a good idea for you yourself to visit the local town hall or council office and to ask about future plans for the neighbourhood. These will only show on the 'local authority searches' if they are well advanced and if they directly affect your particular house. But there may be a vague proposal for a ring road within a few hundred yards of your house. You might want to know of any such plans, however vague, so that you can make up your mind whether they could put you off buying the house.

Inquiries Before Contract

Local authorities supply a great deal of information, yet this is not all you need to know. When solicitors get the draft contract they will ask further questions of the present owner and his or her solicitors. This is usually done on a printed form containing some forty standard questions (not all of them have to be asked about each house). Useful information is provided about the existence of such things as rights of way, woodworm guarantees and fences. In addition, solicitors can ask other relevant questions. For a new house one would ask for a copy of any special conditions the council made when it gave permission to build; or it might be necessary to know whether a garage was put up in recent times. Many solicitors inquire about disputes with neighbours: a buyer might prefer to be warned before he walks into a quarrel over fences or rights of way. Local authorities, owners and solicitors have to answer each question truthfully, but they do not have to volunteer information. Hence the need for so many questions.

Even so, there are a number of things about which you will not normally know before you exchange contracts. Your solicitors may ask whether there are disputes relating to the house, but they cannot ask (and if they did the vendor could refuse to answer) what sort of people the neighbours are, whether quiet, fussy, noisy or given to hysteria. Only time will tell.

The Contract

When all questions have been asked and answered satisfactorily, the next step is the signing and exchange of contracts.

A contract is one of two vital documents required in the buying of every house. The other one, the conveyance or transfer, is dealt with in the next chapter and does not always need to be signed by the buyer (though possible changes are under discussion – autumn 1989).

The exact contents of a contract vary, but it always contains:

the name of the seller and the capacity in which he or she sells (as trustee, owner or executor);

the name of the buyer;

a description of the property (sometimes couched in the florid language used in conveyances: ALL THAT freehold land situate at Bursledon in the County of Hants with the dwellinghouse and garage thereon known as 14 Chestnut Avenue Bursledon aforesaid as the same are shown on the plan annexed hereto and thereon coloured pink and brown);

the price and amount of deposit and probably also a statement whether it is to be held as stakeholders or as agents for the vendor;

the date for completing the purchase;

whether the property is freehold or leasehold. The title of the house should be freehold or a long lease; for a flat or maisonette you want a long lease. Anything else needs careful thought and advice; see a solicitor immediately you know the length of the lease offered to you.

Registered or Unregistered?

The contract also states whether the title to the land is registered or unregistered. Land registration was introduced to simplify the buying and selling of houses. All outright owners without a mortgage on their house have an official land certificate, containing the address of the land, its position on the map, the owner's name and address, and details of special conditions affecting the land. If there is a mortgage, a similar certificate is issued, this time to the lender. A copy of the mortgage is usually bound up with the certificate, which is now known as a charge certificate. Copies of land certificates and charge certificates are available to owners and to their solicitors, and are constantly brought up to date. It is a good system and it is a pity it is spreading so slowly.

Registration of land (although it goes back even further) was generally introduced by the Land Registration Act of 1925, which gave local authorities power to introduce compulsory registration in their area. All land sold after the introduction of compulsory registration has to be put on the Land Register. Virtually all houses in areas such as London, Middlesex, Hastings and Eastbourne are registered, but there are parts of the country which do not yet have compulsory registration, and many more in which some houses are registered and others are not. In those areas, for example Brighton (which introduced compulsory registration in 1965), Bolton (1965), Altrincham (1974) and Manchester (1961), houses have to be registered on the first sale after the system came into force.

All council houses sold under the Housing Act 1980 must be registered even if they are not in a compulsory area. This should give the buyer additional protection: local authority titles are not always clear and straightforward.

Finally, there are the 'Conditions of Sale'. A great many of these, like the rules of cricket or tennis, are there to be referred to if certain contingencies arise. They are laid down once and for all and need not be repeated in every contract any more than the rules of play need to be read out at the start of every game. The contract will say something like: 'The property is sold subject to the National Conditions of sale which shall be deemed to be incorporated in this contract so far as they are not inconsistent with the conditions herein contained.' One condition frequently changed relates to the rate of interest you will have to pay if you don't produce the purchase money on the date fixed for completion.

The contract is usually prepared in duplicate, one copy signed by the vendor, the other by the purchaser. Payment of the 10 per cent deposit and the exchange of the two copies – the seller's with the buyer's – fixes the point of no return. Once contracts are exchanged you are bound in law to go on with your purchase, and the seller is bound to go on with the sale. This is so whether you live or die, whether the house is burnt down and whether you get your mortgage or not. You now know why so much time and effort and heart-searching are required before a contract is signed.

By the time you come to sign the contract you ought to know:

what the local authority has in store for your house;
any unusual disclosures made by the present owner;
how much money you will be able to borrow;
whether you have enough to pay the deposit and the balance;
whether you can afford to run the house;
what your surveyor says about it.

Talk to your solicitor if you are doubtful about any of these points. Sign only when you are satisfied.

Chapter 14

Between Contract and Completion

Do not be surprised if you find that you are more than usually irritable shortly after deciding to buy a house. You will worry about whether the owner is likely to sell to somebody else and will be impatient to get contracts exchanged. You will also worry about your chances of getting a mortgage. At the same time you will almost certainly like the house less well on your second visit than on your first, you may have a surveyor's report showing that it is far from perfect, and you may wonder whether it is worth sinking so much money in it. These are anxious days, but if you put yourself in the hands of a good solicitor and a good surveyor you should come through safely.

Once you have made the momentous decision and have exchanged contracts, the air clears. You are now in a similar position to the man who is engaged to be married: he does not at this stage have a wife, and you do not have a house, but both of you have taken on some of the responsibilities of your future state. Unlike an engagement, however, the exchange of contracts on a house tends to take place in the absence of those chiefly affected. The contract is typed out in duplicate, you sign one copy and the seller signs the other. You give yours to your solicitor with the 10 per cent deposit, and carry on with something else. They send contract and deposit to the seller's solicitors, who in exchange send the copy signed by their client.

Contracts are 'exchanged' at the precise point when the seller's copy is posted to the buyer's solicitor, or when both solicitors agree on the telephone that this is the moment. If you allow for your purchase being part of a longish chain of other purchases, all needing to complete their buying and selling on the same day, you can see that even over the telephone it can take several hours to exchange contracts. All solicitors along the chain have to be in a position to say: Yes, Thursday the 31st will be OK for completion.

Once contracts are exchanged both sides are bound. What is more, the house is now formally yours, though you have no right to occupy it till you have paid the balance of the purchase price.

As the house is yours the sellers have to take good care of your property. If they break a window, or back a car into the garden fence, they have to mend it. You, on the other hand, will suffer if the house burns down, if a burglar breaks the windows or a storm takes off the roof. You will nevertheless have to go on with your purchase. This is why your solicitors insure the house as a matter of course as soon as contracts are exchanged. When there is a mortgage, the lender usually insists on handling the insurance, though you can suggest an insurance company. Most people take out a comprehensive insurance policy, and many building societies insist on this, though a few are satisfied if you insure against fire risk only.

House Insurance

If you have a choice it is worth shopping around: some policies are slightly more 'comprehensive' than others, and some companies offer a 'no-claims bonus' in the form of a free renewal every sixth year if there have been no claims during the previous five years.

A comprehensive policy should include insurance against:

fire, explosion, lightning, earthquake and subsidence;
all types of theft;
storms, burst pipes and leaking fuel tanks or washing machines;
aeroplanes or cars (other than your own) crashing into the building;
broken washbasins or fixed glass;
damage to underground cables and pipes;
architects', surveyors' and legal fees (see over);

    removal of debris;
    injury or damage to strangers (e.g. from a falling roof tile).

Most policies, though including storm damage and damage
caused by water, make the owner bear the first portion of
expense. For an extra premium that limit can be removed.

The fact that architects' fees etc. are included may reassure
you rather more than it ought to. Imagine that the house is
totally destroyed by fire: the most the insurance company
would pay is the amount for which you have insured. Out of
this you would have to remove debris, redesign and rebuild
the house. It is therefore wise to add 15 per cent to the amount
for which you would otherwise insure. Some companies, to
make this difficulty clear, offer architects' fees etc. as an additional insurance.

How much to insure for? With an average house you won't
go far wrong if you insure for about the amount you pay for
the house. If you are buying at a bargain price, you may wish
to insure for rather more. In any event, review the insurance
every few years. It should always be high enough for the
house to be completely rebuilt in case of disaster. To allow for
the rise in building costs your insurance company may well
automatically increase the sum insured each year. If not,
remember to check when you get your premium demand: how
much are you insured for? Some mortgages collect house-
insurance premiums once a year, others spread premiums
over the whole year – adding one twelfth to each monthly
mortgage demand. If yours does this, it is easy to forget to
check from time to time how much you are insured for.
Lenders insist on a minimum insurance cover, but you yourself
can always go higher. Another insurance worth thinking
about – though not cheap – pays your mortgage payments if
you become ill or unemployed for a period. Look carefully at
the terms offered: compensation payments will probably be for
a fairly limited period. For example, they may start after two
months and go on for up to nine months of disability.

While I am dealing with the gloomy side: what would
happen to your house if the owner or a member of his or her
family died before completion? The sale would have to go on,
however inconvenient this might be for the survivors. Your

contract, once made, does not depend on the owner living to complete the sale. If the owner died you would have to wait for personal representatives to be appointed, and you would then buy the house from them.

Nor does the purchaser's death end a contract to buy a house. Anyone who is buying with the aid of an endowment policy would therefore do well to take out the policy as soon as contracts are exchanged. The policy would mature on the death of the purchaser and would provide the purchase money. And of course the house could always be resold if it were no longer suitable for the buyer's family.

For those borrowing money under a repayment mortgage, a mortgage protection policy is useful, particularly while there are dependent children (see also p. 40).

Even if there is no insurance policy there is a way out. This is what happened in Laura Piper's family: her brother George was killed in a car crash two days after signing the contract for a new house. George's widow could not afford the house. She put it into the hands of estate agents, who found another buyer for the house. Through her solicitor she applied for probate of George's will and after a few weeks she sold the house as his executor without losing too much money over it.

Legal Documents

The Title Deeds

Your solicitors will have a copy of the entries on the Land Register affecting your new house (pp. 144–6) and an authority to inspect the original. Armed with these two documents, your solicitors can check whether the copy is accurate and whether it refers to the same house and the same owner as the contract, and can make sure that there are no restrictions of which they were not told before, and that the present owner's mortgage will be paid off before you take over ownership.

Not every investigation of title, even of registered land, is so simple. Where there is, for example, a new housing estate with

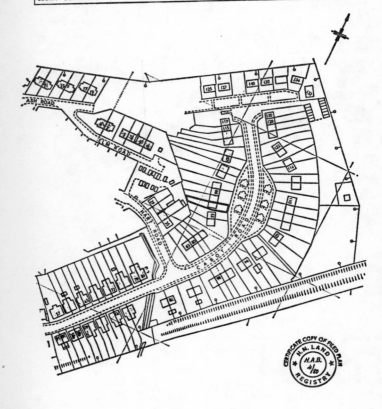

(Reproduced by kind permission of the Chief Land Registrar)

H.M. LAND REGISTRY

| Edition | 1 | opened | 14.4.1980 | TITLE NUMBER | BLK0009 | This register consists of | 2 | pages |

A. PROPERTY REGISTER

containing the description of the registered land and the estate comprised in the Title

COUNTY	DISTRICT
BLANKSHIRE	BROXMORE

The Freehold land shown and edged with red on the plan of the above Title filed at the Registry registered on 14 April 1980 known as 95 Cabot Road.

B. PROPRIETORSHIP REGISTER

stating nature of the Title, name, address and description of the proprietor of the land and any entries affecting the right of disposing thereof

TITLE ABSOLUTE

Entry number	Proprietor, etc.
1.	MICHAEL BENNETT Plumber and MARY SUSAN BENNETT his wife both of 95 Cabot Road, Broxmore, Blankshire, registered on 14 April 1980.
2.	RESTRICTION registered on 14 April 1980. No disposition by one proprietor of the land (being the survivor of joint proprietors and not being a trust corporation) under which capital money arises is to be registered except under an order of the registrar or of the Court.

Demand No. 8037440 11/79 W & W Ltd. 1314

Register Model III

Any entries struck through are no longer subsisting

Page 2   TITLE NUMBER BLK0009

	C. CHARGES REGISTER	
	containing charges, incumbrances etc., adversely affecting the land and registered dealings therewith	
Entry number	The date at the beginning of each entry is the date on which the entry was made on this edition of the register	Remarks
1.	14 April 1980—A Conveyance dated 30 September 1934 and made between (1) Mary Brown (Vendor) and (2) Harold Robins (Purchaser) contains the following covenants:—	
	"The Purchaser hereby covenants with the Vendor for the benefit of her adjoining land known as 85, 87, 89, 91 and 93 Cabot Road to observe and perform the stipulations and conditions contained in the Schedule hereto:—	
	<u>THE SCHEDULE before referred to</u>	
	1. No building to be erected on the land shall be used other than as a private dwellinghouse.	
	2. No building to be erected as aforesaid shall be converted into or used as flats, maisonettes or separate tenements or as a boarding house.	
	3. The garden ground of the premises shall at all times be kept in neat and proper order and condition and shall not be converted to any other use whatsoever.	
	4. Nothing shall be done or permitted on the premises which may be a nuisance or annoyance to the adjoining houses or to the neighbourhood."	
2.	14 April 1980—CHARGE dated 2 April 1980 registered on 14 April 1980 to secure the moneys including the further advances therein mentioned.	
3.	PROPRIETOR—BLANKSHIRE BUILDING SOCIETY of 27 High Street, Broxmore, Blankshire, registered on 14 April 1980.	

Any entries struck through are no longer subsisting

leases to each new owner, a sale by an executor or a sale of a small portion of a large estate, the documents can be voluminous and awkward to examine. This is your solicitors' problem, not yours, but it may have some influence on the fees you have to pay.

When the title is not registered, there is every chance that the documents, even in a simple case, will be lengthy and numerous. You are entitled to know the continuous history of the house: who sold it to whom and for how much, who took it on whose death, whether it was mortgaged and if every mortgage was paid off. To find out, your solicitors go through the title deeds for at least the last fifteen years. One of the points they check is whether you are getting the right house. This is quite easy if the house has always been known by the same number and the street by the same name. But in our once rural country this cannot be taken for granted. Many years ago a piece of rural England, part of a county largely owned by one of the big landowning families, was charged with providing pin money for one of the daughters on her marriage. Later she released some of that land to her youngest son, who exchanged it for another piece of land belonging to his elder brother. True to the highest family traditions both brothers had long and almost identical names. One brother went on farming the land and left it to his son, who left it to his own son who used some of the land to pay death duties and sold the rest to a builder. The other brother went mad, his land had to be looked after by someone else and sold as the need arose. Some of it was sold to the same builder, who eventually sold part of his land to another builder, who put up twenty-seven semi-detached houses. If you are buying a semi-detached house, you want to be sure it is one of the twenty-seven and not a house wrongfully built on land belonging to someone else. Investigating a title of this sort is detective work. Similar problems may be involved in checking the credentials of the sellers. Are they the owners of the house? If not, how did they acquire the right to sell? They may be the owner's executor – in which case all is well – or they may be confidence tricksters – in which case it is not.

In the course of investigating the title your solicitors will probably fire another list of questions at the vendor's solicitors. These are called 'Requisitions on Title' and are aimed at clearing up all doubts which may arise on investigating the title deeds. At the same time they will also find out where the sale is going to be completed and what banker's drafts will be needed (more about both these below).

Form 19(JP)

HM Land Registry

Land Registration Acts, 1925 to 1971

Stamp pursuant to section 28 of the Finance Act 1931 to be impressed here	*When the transfer attracts Inland Revenue duty, the stamps should be impressed here before lodging the transfer for registration.*

(1) For a transfer to a sole proprietor use printed form 19.

(¹) TRANSFER OF WHOLE TO JOINT PROPRIETORS
(Freehold or Leasehold)
(Rules 98 or 115, Land Registration Rules 1925)

County and district (or London borough) } Blankshire, Broxmore

Title number(s) BLK0009

Property .... 95 Cabot Road

Date .... 19 ...... In consideration of ... TWENTY-EIGHT THOUSAND ----

(2) Strike out if not required

----------------pounds (£ 28,000.00-------) (²)*the receipt whereof is hereby acknowledged*

(3) In BLOCK LETTERS, enter full name(s), postal address(es) and occupation(s) of the proprietor(s) of the land

(³)I/We _ Michael Bennett of 95 Cabot Road,

Broxmore, Blankshire

(4) If desired, or otherwise as the case may be (see rules 76 and 77)

(⁴)*as beneficial owner(s)* hereby transfer to:

(5) In BLOCK LETTERS, enter full name(s), postal address(es) and occupation(s) of the transferee(s) for entry on the register

(⁵)

Thomas Alexander Jones and May Jones both of 10 Mildert Walk, Durham

(6) Any special clause should be entered here

(7) A transfer for charitable uses should follow form 36 (see rules 121 and 122).

the land comprised in the title(s) above mentioned (⁶) (⁷)

(8) Delete the inappropriate alternative

The transferees declare that the survivor of them(⁸) ~~can~~ ——— give a valid receipt for capital money arising ~~XXRRXX~~ on a disposition of the land.

(9) If a certificate of value for the purposes of the Stamp Act 1891 and amending Acts is not required this paragraph should be deleted

(⁹)*It is hereby certified that the transaction hereby effected does not form part of a larger transaction or series of transactions in respect of which the amount or value or aggregate amount or value of the consideration exceeds £ 30,000*

(10) This transfer must be executed by the transferees as well as the transferor

(¹⁰) Signed, sealed and delivered by the said
    MICHAEL BENNETT |

                                                            (Seal)

in the presence of |

Name

Address

Occupation

This form of transfer has been reproduced by the kind permission of Oyez Publishing Ltd.

The Transfer or Conveyance

When they are satisfied about the title, your solicitors prepare the document which will transfer the ownership of the house from its present owner to you. As a general rule a conveyance (of unregistered land) (see p. 151) is a more complex document than a transfer (of registered) (see opposite).

When more than one person is buying, the words 'as beneficial joint tenants' are sometimes added after the names of the new owners. These words mean that on the death of one of them the other (or others) will get the house. But the phrase is not essential: in the transfer above, on the death of either Tom or May the house will automatically pass to the survivors. (See also pp. 132–3 for the pros and cons of joint ownership).

It is quite possible for people to buy jointly but to keep their interests separated. Two brothers, for example, might buy a house and each want to leave his share to his wife. Their transfer would have to include words such as 'as beneficial tenants in common'. Clause 2 in the land certificate on pp. 144–6 shows that the previous owners bought as tenants in common.

The clause beginning 'It is hereby certified ...' is vital. Without it a transfer or conveyance has to bear stamp duty. (For details of exemption from stamp duty, see pp. 62–3.)

Conveyances of unregistered land (p. 151) follow a set pattern. After the names and addresses of seller and buyer, the part beginning WHEREAS ... tells of any important events which have happened since the last conveyance – in the present case very little. Had the last owner died, this would be recounted there with the name of his executor and the date of probate and would explain why the executor rather than the last owner was selling.

NOW THIS DEED ... signifies the beginning of the conveyance proper: first, the price, then whether the owner sells his own or somebody else's property, next a description of what he is selling.

TO HOLD starts the part showing whether the buyer is getting freehold or leasehold ('in fee simple' means he is buying freehold) and whether there are special rules affecting the house. These are the 'restrictions and stipulations contained in the ... Conveyance'. They might say, for example, that the house is to be used only as a private residence and not for business, or that no washing may be put out on Sundays.

The conveyance will be shown to Smith's solicitors in draft; they may suggest alterations, and after the draft has been agreed between solicitors and typed on very strong paper or parchment (it will have to last for many years), it is sent to John Smith to sign in the presence of a witness. After John Smith has signed, the last clause looks like this:

SIGNED SEALED AND DELIVERED by
the said JOHN SMITH in the
presence of: } *J. Smith*

T. Hubbard

2 The Crossroads
Sarisbury, Hants
Engineer

A small red wafer seal will be stuck to the right of Mr Smith's signature. There is no magic about these positions, but they make for order. In the simplest cases the buyer need not sign the transfer or conveyance; they are signed merely by the seller. A mortgage, on the other hand, always needs the signature of the borrower.

The Mortgage

Some mortgage documents are long and complicated. Others are on a single page handsomely subdivided, and refer to a book of rules which you are supposed to study but probably won't. The points of importance to the house-buyer (called 'the Borrower' in the mortgage) are the amount of the monthly or quarterly payments, and the knowledge that the mortgage gives the lender formidable powers to enforce regular payment. In the last resort a lender can sell a house over a defaulting borrower's head. What is more, this happens

THIS CONVEYANCE is made the   day of
19   BETWEEN   JOHN SMITH of 40 Fareham Road Southampton in the County of
Hants (hereinafter called 'the Vendor') of the one part and PETER PIPER of
25 The Market Petersfield in the said County of Hants (hereinafter called
'the Purchaser') of the other part

W H E R E A S:

> The Vendor is seized of the property hereinafter described for
> an estate in fee simple in possession free from encumbrances
> and has agreed to sell the same for a like estate to the
> Purchaser for the sum of £...000

> **NOW THIS DEED W I T N E S S E T H :**

That in pursuance of the said agreement and in consideration of the sum
of......thousand Pounds (£...000) now paid by the Purchaser to the Vendor
(the receipt whereof the Vendor hereby acknowledges) the Vendor as
BENEFICIAL OWNER hereby CONVEYS UNTO the Purchaser ALL THAT messuage or
dwellinghouse outbuildings and land situate in the Parish of Bursledon in
the County of Hants and known as 14 Chestnut Avenue Bursledon aforesaid as
the same is for the purposes of identification only delineated on the plan
drawn hereon and thereon coloured pink TO HOLD the same unto the Purchaser
in fee simple subject to the restrictions and stipulations contained in the
Schedule to a Conveyance dated the 1st day of November 1902 and made
between County Developments Limited of the one part and Roderick Random of
the other part so far as the same are still subsisting and capable of being
enforced.
IT IS HEREBY CERTIFIED that the transaction hereby effected does not form
part of a larger transaction or series of transactions in respect of which
the amount or value or aggregate amount or value of the consideration
exceeds £...000.
IN WITNESS whereof the Vendor has hereunto set his hand and seal the day
and year first above written.
SIGNED SEALED AND DELIVERED)
by the said JOHN SMITH in)
the presence of:)

after the borrower has been taken to court, at his own expense. Consider taking out insurance against illness and unemployment (see p.142).

Within a few days of completing the house purchase you will be told the day of the month when your mortgage payments are due. It is a good idea to arrange with your bank to pay the mortgage each month by banker's order or direct debit. This avoids the risk of the payment being overlooked. The bank, of course, can pay only if there is enough money in the account: whatever else you have to cut down on, be sure to keep the account healthy. If you have arranged for direct debit payments, remember when the lenders told you they would go up. Even the most careful plans can be upset by illness, unemployment or divorce. Here are some hints which may help should you strike unlucky:

(1) Tell the mortgagees what has happened and ask whether for a limited time they will let you pay less. Building societies and banks are often prepared to let you pay the interest only, and not to make repayments of capital. Even these payments may be high, but every little will help.

(2) If you are out of work for a long time, allow your capital (excluding the house) to drop below £3,000 and apply for supplementary benefit. The Department of Social Security, though it does not pay endowment premiums, can probably help pay the mortgage interest.

(3) If the drop in income is permanent, ask the building society whether they will extend the mortgage (say, from twenty-five to thirty years), thus reducing your monthly payments.

(4) Reputable lenders much prefer their mortgage money to remain in your house, rather than get a bad name for making people homeless when they fall on hard times. Be open with your building society and you will find them understanding. What you must avoid at all cost is to fall behind, without explanation, in the forlorn hope that they will not notice. They always do.

(5) Reputable lenders sometimes sell their business and with it your mortgage to less reputable ones who put up mortgage interest by more than a fair degree. Try to persuade one of the big banks or building societies to take over your mortgage if

this should happen to you. If you have been conscientious with payments in the past, they may be prepared to take over.

(6) If the worst comes to the worst, and the mortgagees want their money and you have no way of finding it, remember: you cannot be evicted without a court order. Go to the court on the day of the hearing and explain why you have not been paying and how you propose to get straight again. The court can allow a reasonable time for you to pay off arrears or to give you a chance of selling the house and getting a less expensive one.

Chapter 15

Preparing Your Move

The contract usually fixes a date for completion, about four weeks ahead, to give everyone time to make final arrangements.

You and the Seller

Once contracts have been exchanged, sellers – even those who previously kept you very much at arm's length – usually become friendly and helpful. You may get useful information about school, church, doctor, butcher, newspaper shop and others.

Settle with the owner whether gas, electricity and water are or are not to be cut off. In winter it is wise to turn off water at the mains if the house is to be unoccupied for even a short period. If you move in on the day the seller moves out, much trouble can be saved by leaving all supplies connected. In that case sign agreements with the Gas and Electricity Boards before you move in, but make it clear that you will move – and be responsible for supplies – on, say, the 15th and not before. Remind the owner to have the meter read before the sale. You may also be able to take over the telephone.

The seller is, up to the date of the sale, responsible for all the outgoings on the house from rates to newspapers. It is up to the seller to cancel milk, electricity, etc., and for you, the buyer, to arrange your own supplies.

The Seller and His Solicitor

Rates, water rates and ground rent continue, whoever owns the house. But the old owner does not have to pay the new one's rates. He could ask the council for a refund, but often his solicitor, to save him trouble, works out exactly how much is due by the old owner and how much by the new, and adjusts the figure on completion. If the old owner has paid beyond the date of sale, he gets a proportion back; if it is the other way round, he either pays, or makes an allowance on completion.

Whatever method is used, the new owner is responsible for rates and water rates from completion of the purchase. If you are not moving in for some time after buying, tell the council, because you may not have to pay rates while the house is empty.*

Apart from rates (and ground rent and insurance in a leasehold house or flat) the seller's solicitors find out from the lenders exactly how much is needed to repay the mortgage on the completion date. This is repaid when you buy the house, and you are not concerned with it.

After this the vendor's solicitor prepares a 'completion statement' and sends it to your solicitor. A traditional completion statement looks something like this:

re 14 Chestnut Avenue, Bursledon
Completion statement as at 1st May 19. .

Purchase price	£30,000.00
Less deposit already paid	£3,000.00
	—————
	£27,000.00

Deduct proportion of General Rate
    1.4 to 30.4 (30 days)
    at £400 per year   £32.87

—————
£26,967.13

(This means that the vendor has paid rates up to 31 March, but not beyond.)

---

* This is relevant only until the community charge has replaced domestic rates.

Add proportion of water rate
　　　1.5 to 30.6 (61 days)
　　　at £36 per year　　　　　　　　　　　　　　　　£6.02
　　　　　　　　　　　　　　　　　　　　　　　　　————

Amount payable on completion　　　　　　　　　£26,973.15

(*Vendor has paid water rate in advance and gets back a proportion for the period after the house is no longer his.*)

Please supply two banker's drafts:

　　　£13,194.12 in favour of　　　　　　(vendor's building society)
　　　£13,779.03 in favour of　　　　　　　　(vendor's solicitors)

　　　————
　　　£26,973.15
　　　————

Note: Increasingly, solicitors try to obtain apportioned figures direct from the rates department and the Water Board; the result is that the rates will not figure in the amount you pay on completion. Whichever method is used, you are not responsible for the old owner's rate or water rate. Your responsibility starts when you become the owner of the house.

Your Solicitors (1)

At this stage, your solicitors will:

　　　check the completion statement for errors of addition;
　　　prepare their bill of costs and send it to you;
　　　find out exactly how much money your lenders will provide on completion, after allowing for stamp duties, legal fees, guarantee policy premium, retention for repairs, final inspection fee, etc. – these vary from case to case.

When they have all the figures, they send you a statement explaining how much they need from you. They will want the amount on the completion statement, plus their costs, stamp duties, Land Registry fees, etc, less the amount which will come from the lenders. The solicitors will also tell you whether they need a cheque or a banker's draft from you.

You (1)

You will probably have to visit your solicitor to sign the mortgage, possibly also the conveyance or transfer.

If they tell you that the conveyance or transfer needs your signature, do not delay. You will have to sign before the seller can sign, so get the document back into the hands of your solicitors as quickly as possible.

If you think you are likely to be away when all this is happening, it is a good idea to give your solicitors plenty of warning.

If you get mortgage or conveyance or transfer through the post, do make a point of signing where you are asked to sign. The buyer usually signs to the right of the small clause which starts: SIGNED ... and contains his name. The witness to the signature signs underneath that clause, adding his or her address and occupation after the signature. You don't (see p. 151). One or two lending institutions, to show how thoroughly modern they are, have reversed the order. The borrower signs on the left, the witness on the right – both on the same line. One good look at the end of the mortgage will tell what is expected of you.

Remember that a cheque may need up to ten days to be cleared, so be sure to send the money in good time to your solicitors.

If there is not enough time, your solicitor will ask you for a banker's draft – a glorified cheque, signed by the bank manager. To get a banker's draft, you draw a cheque on your own bank, hand it to the branch where you keep your account, and ask the bank to make out a banker's draft. This takes only a few minutes. The bank will charge a small fee.

Your Solicitors (2)

A few days before completion, your solicitors make a search at the Land Registry or the Land Charges Registry.

The Land Registry search is a simple and effective check on

your title to the house, and makes sure that the house is not going to be sold to two people at once. If the search is clear, it not only reassures you that no one has tried to snatch ownership from you, it goes further and promises that for fourteen working days from the date of your search the Land Registry will not deal with anyone else. This gives your solicitors time to complete the purchase, stamp the papers and lodge them with the Registry, who then put your name on the Register as that of the new owner. No one else has a chance of dishonestly slipping in. For a house with unregistered title a similar search is made at the Land Charges Registry. The solicitors acting for your mortgagees will also make a search to find out whether you have gone bankrupt. If you have, you will not get your mortgage.

With luck your solicitors will, on the day before completion, have the completion money from the lender and from you, cleared and available to draw against. The completion statement tells them whether the purchase money is to be paid in one sum to the seller's solicitors or partly to them and partly to the seller's own lenders. As soon as all the money is in their hands, your solicitors finalize the completion of your purchase, either by transferring the money to the seller's solicitors' bank or by going to their office armed with banker's drafts.

Chains

Not what they use to stop you from committing murder if you can't get into your new house on the due date. We talk of chains when several people have to buy and sell their houses on the same day. You cannot buy your new house and move in till you have the money for your old house. The people who are buying your old house cannot do so till they have been paid by the people who are buying theirs. And so on . . . If there is a breakdown somewhere, a large number of people can be in difficulty.

There are those who blame the solicitors and sit back in anger. More realistically, you can plan for such emergencies and go on hoping they will not happen. Miraculously, the majority of completions take place on the intended day.

How to Cope with Delay

Obviously you will do all you can to avoid delay. Make sure your solicitors know where to get hold of you, that you know how much money is needed from you, and get the right amount into the hands of your solicitor in time. Problems sometimes arise because documents get lost or are delayed in the post. It is hoped that local authorities, land registries and building societies will soon all communicate with solicitors by computer and that this will simplify the procedure somewhat. Keep your fingers crossed! When the computer breaks down, we shall no doubt long for the good old days when letters, more often than not, reached their proper destination.

Emergency No. 1: You Cannot Get into Your New House

The most likely cause of trouble is money: someone along the line does not have enough money to complete on time. If your sellers cannot move to their new house they may decide to stay put, and you cannot move into their old one. You can either react by also staying put, or, if you have planned ahead, move in with friends or relations for a few days. If you yourself make it clear that you are ready to complete your purchase, you will neither pay interest to your seller for later completion, nor will you start paying interest on your new mortgage if the delay is at all prolonged. Unfortunately, the seller will not owe you compensation either, unless the delay is so long that completion notices have been served. At the same time, by moving out and completing the sale of your old house you will have paid off your old mortgage and will have a large sum of money in the bank.

Emergency No. 2: You Cannot Complete Your own Purchase on Time

Here again, the most likely reason is money: your mortgage cheque or your own cheque for the balance has not been cleared, or your buyer has been held up. If this cannot be overcome in a day, the quickest solution probably is a bridging loan from your bank. Weigh up the cost of such a loan against the inconvenience of changing your plans and the cost of completing late. This cost depends on how much interest you save on *not* taking out your new mortgage and how much interest you have to pay for not buying on the date fixed for completion. Your solicitors can help with the calculations. At present, delayed completion is more expensive for frustrated buyers than for sellers, who have at least a fortnight's grace. There is a move afoot to make sellers, too, pay compensation to the buyer for every day's delay caused by them. It will depend on the state of the housing market whether the idea catches on.

Moving Before Completion

It is usually a term of the contract that 'vacant possession shall be given on completion', which means that the purchaser gets the key to the house against the purchase money. Occasionally, the old owner moves out before completion and, rather than leave the house empty, allows the new owner to move in before the purchase money is ready. This seemingly simple courtesy can have serious legal results for sellers. Do not, therefore, consider them unreasonable if, after taking advice from their solicitor, they say No to a request to move in early.

However, some owners will allow purchasers in. Usually this is on terms that the buyer pays all outgoings from the time of moving in and pays interest on the purchase money.

It is often as cheap to borrow money and to complete earlier, or to store your furniture and stay with friends for a month.

If you are lucky, the old owner may allow you to prepare your move some days ahead, without your having to pay. You may be allowed to do repairs, or start painting, so long as you give your word not to move in before the completion date.

Or, you may have a few days after completion while the new home is being cleaned up, carpets are fitted, alterations put in hand. But far more often everything has to be done on one day: you arrive, put down floor tiles and carpets as you go along, swiftly, so that the heavy pieces of furniture can come next and you can start emptying boxes and filling cupboards. Such a move repays careful preparation.

You (2): Preparing Your Move

Removal costs vary; it is worth getting several estimates. As well as comparing prices, try to get a personal recommendation. Some removers are very much more skilful, quick and considerate than others.

If you are moving from a big city to the provinces, you often do better to look for a remover in the smaller place: many firms have loads to go to London and but for your move might have to return empty. They will probably charge less for the move than a London firm. Also, move in the middle of the week, in the middle of the month, if you can. Removal firms get very busy on Fridays and at the beginning and end of the month. Take off, say, Thursday, to move. Ignore the mess while you are at work on Friday and spend the weekend getting settled. It is less exhausting and probably cheaper.

You don't necessarily save money by doing your own packing – ask the removal firm about this. Alternatively, go the whole hog and tackle the move yourself (see p. 165 for the grisly experience of the author). To do this, you need (1) a van; (2) a driver with the appropriate driving licence; (3) able-bodied and skilful helpers.

A small (30 cwt) van is useful for a move over a short distance; you can move one or two rooms at a time. For longer distances, several journeys are expensive and time-consuming. Bear in mind, though, that to drive a large van you need an HGV licence.

Make sure that the driver can handle a van and that both driver and furniture are insured as far as possible. If you are able to borrow the van from a friend, check both the friend's and your own car insurance – one or other may well cover the van. If you hire a van, check with the hire company.

If you hire a van, it is a good idea to pick it up early enough for a trial run. A van in bad shape can throw a spanner in the works. You need all your time and energy for the move and have none to spare trying to repair a van that has not been overhauled before you receive it.

The move will go considerably more smoothly if you have taken care of certain things beforehand.

Furniture insurance: Tell you insurance company when you intend to move and ask them to insure your chattels during the removal and at your new address. If you want to change insurance companies, this is a good moment: tell the old one to cancel your policy as from the day after you leave and to refund the rest of the year's premium. Ask the new company to insure the furniture in transit and at the new house.

Gas and electricity: Unless your new house is going to be all electric, write to both Area Boards asking them to lay on supplies. When the moving day has been fixed, arrange for the Board to send a fitter to the new house, to connect the cooker on that day. Also arrange for your own cooker to be disconnected and your meters to be read. Give the Board as much notice as you can. They often find it unbelievably difficult to disconnect and reconnect a cooker on one and the same day.

Telephone: It is easy to have your old telephone cut off, but it can be difficult and frustratingly slow to get a telephone in your new home. Try to take over the seller's telephone; installing a new one is expensive and often takes time. Some telephone managers, far from eager to do business, convey the impression that you are being greedy and unreasonable in wanting a telephone ready and functioning when you move in. Do not be disheartened but do allow time for making arrangements.

Letters: Arrange for the Post Office to forward them to your new address. The Post Office will supply a form for you to fill in and return.

Tell your friends: To be on the safe side, send your change of address to friends, bank, etc – to anyone whose letters you value.

School: If the move means a change of school for your children, do not forget to tell the new Education Authority when they will be starting.

Food: Even if there is not time for a visit to the area, try to find out where the nearest shops are. Perhaps the seller will lay on milk at least for the first day.

Keys: Persuade the owner to leave all the keys when he or she moves out, and arrange where to pick them up. The most convenient method is to leave one key with the estate agents if they are nearby, or with a neighbour. The remaining keys are often left on the mantelpiece. You are not entitled to a key till you have completed the purchase.

Most important: Arrange who is to be where on moving day. Your children will probably have the day off school, but anyone under fifteen is likely to get weary long before the move is complete. (So, for that matter, will you, but bear up, you don't have to move every day.) Overrule the children's protests and arrange for them to spend the day with some fond relation. If possible, let them take all pets; this has the double merit of keeping the pets out of the way and stopping the children from feeling unwanted.

Before you usher them out, ask the children to prepare number cards, one for each room in the new house. Also lay in a box of drawing pins or sticky tape and a piece of chalk. Give each room in the new house a number, and mark each piece of furniture and every heavy box or trunk with the appropriate number. This prevents grandfather's bed from landing up in the nursery while your back is turned.

Moving Day

Do not have too many helpers. The ideal number is three to four: two knowledgeable members of your household and one friend or possibly two, experienced in moving house. Try to have one knowledgeable member of the household in the old house and one in the new to deal with unforeseen queries. No move is without them: do the goldfish stay in the pond or come with you? What happens to the pelmets, or dustbins? What about the suit still at the dry cleaner's, and the card for Aunt Lucy's eightieth birthday on the mantelpiece? A helpful stranger might post it, not knowing that the card had been written a year earlier and the old lady had passed away in the meantime.

While you are waiting for the removal van, you will have time for a last nostalgic look round the house. Check whether you have marked all pieces of furniture with room numbers for the new house. Keep some spare chalk to mark the chests which the removal men will bring for china, etc. Do not trouble to pack china or glass, unless you are convinced that you are better at packing than they are. They will come armed with tea chests and packing material.

Removers have an uncanny knack of taking apart large pieces of furniture, such as wardrobes and cupboards. For this reason, clothes as well as sweaters, shoes and other articles kept on shelves inside your wardrobe usually travel better in trunks. Stuff kept in drawers, on the other hand, can travel without being shifted.

The contents of drawers in fitted cupboards are easily forgotten, so are things in the attic, garden, outhouses and anywhere above eye level. This is where an experienced member of the household can prove his or her mettle. They will also make sure that you leave behind all the bits and pieces which you have sold, or promised to leave for the new owner.

The other experienced member will have found out where the nearest phone box is, and made sure that there will be parking space for the removal van outside the new house. He or she will, if possible, arrive ahead of the van, having brought along:

(1) the numbered cards and drawing pins or sticky tape. One card should be fixed to each door. If the helper is at all absent-minded, or if the house has many rooms, prepare a plan showing which room is to have what number, otherwise the piano might yet turn up in the bedroom and the wardrobe in the dining room;

(2) a broom, bucket and rough cleaning materials. Even if the house is left beautifully clean, the helper will feel less lonely if some cleaning can be done while waiting for the removal van;

(3) a toilet roll, towel and soap;

(4) a number of coins for telephoning, even if you have arranged to take over the telephone in the house. Telephones have been known to break down;

(5) a camping stove if you have one or can borrow one, with a

kettle, several mugs and all that is needed for morale-raising cups of tea while you are waiting. Indeed you might as well play safe and allow for the cooker not being reconnected on the day of your move. This can be borne more equably if your family is not on a strict diet of exclusively cold food.

The experienced member will check whether the seller has left behind all the things included in the sale, and will rejoice in any he or she finds without having to pay for them. Many owners abandon lino and vinyl (they move very badly), curtain rails and light fittings. But should you find lampshades or lawn mowers it would be better to put them on one side and find out whether the previous owners meant to leave them or merely forgot them. You will probably have asked for their new address – you are bound to get letters addressed to them even if they made arrangements with the Post Office.

Once the removal men arrive things tend to move swiftly. Before long the floor will be littered with shoes, books, detergent, frozen peas, light bulbs, blankets and cat food. Workmen who swore they could not fit you in for a fortnight will appear; so will goods which you may or may not have ordered.

Do-It-Yourself Move

In our family we can muster six able-bodied adults and are blessed with practical and helpful friends: we have recently tackled several moves which, though exhausting, were also quite fun and the occasion for a family reunion. We none of us have an HGV licence nor have we tackled long-distance moves. Whoever comes furthest usually brings the hired van, saving his rail fare. To get a good van we have found a matter of trial and error. If you cannot get a personal recommendation, the Yellow Pages in your telephone directory are as good a guide as any. Most firms give a choice between a daily all-in charge, and a lower charge plus so much per mile. For short-distance moves, it is usually cheaper to pay mileage.

For about a fortnight before the move we collect cardboard boxes from our supermarket and fill them up gradually. We have learnt the hard way that very large boxes may be suitable for large quantities of cornflakes but will collapse if filled with clothes, books or china. Middle-sized boxes are best. We pack every piece of glass and china separately in newspaper. This is a bore and takes up a lot of time and space. But we have never yet broken anything.

Hi-fi equipment, records and delicate glass, etc., do of course prefer the back seat of a car to any van, however carefully driven. If time allows, two of us have decorated at least the main living room before the big move. Very often, of course, time does not allow, and everything has to be done in one day. In that case two of us start cleaning up and, with luck, painting one room as soon as we can get into the new house.

The movers at the old house must remember to start by loading the light articles and end up with the heavy ones, leaving the carpet until the end. If you move one room at a time, this happens almost automatically. When you arrive at the new house, you want the carpet out first, next you want to get at the sideboard without having to lift a lot of boxes off first. Some of the furniture will have been taken to pieces – this is fine if you are good at jigsaw puzzles and have a strong nerve. I have neither and usually panic at this stage. A chorus of 'Don't worry' sends me off to make yet another cup of tea for everyone.

One helper will in any event spend most of the day preparing and clearing away meals, plus cleaning and putting stuff away in cupboards. We have found it a good idea to concentrate on getting one, or possibly two, rooms into a reasonable state by the evening. One habitable room in contrast with others in a state of chaos makes us feel much better than several rooms all vaguely coming along. When you sit down to your well-deserved evening meal it also helps if you have made sure of a bed for the night. Well, if not a bed, at least a mattress; and if not a mattress, some clear floor space and a blanket. Next time, you may decide, you will go away and leave the job to the most highly recommended firm of removers you can find.

One ray of light: you do not have to concern yourself with the completion of the house purchase. This is in the hands of your solicitors and of the other lawyers involved: an ordinary completion may need as many as four.

The Solicitors

The odds are that the money to pay for your house (particularly if you are selling one to buy another) is not available until some time on the day of completion. If all solicitors and banks involved in the transaction are in one area, money and documents can be exchanged personally at the office of the seller's solicitors or that of the seller's mortgagee. The one who has the title deeds traditionally gets all other solicitors to call on them for completion of the sale. In modern conditions this is not often practicable, so all firms prepare by checking deeds beforehand, promising to send them on receipt of the purchase price and sending moneys by telegraphic transfer via their banks.

Completion can be very involved if you are one of a chain of people who all need to sell and buy on the same day, possibly in different parts of the country. Much depends on very careful preparation and on the bank getting the money transferred quickly.

Solicitors usually manage to get everyone fixed up. The house key is sometimes handed over on completion, but more often it is left with either an estate agent or with neighbours of the seller; if necessary the seller's solicitor rings up to say it is in order for the key to be handed over to you.

From that moment onwards the house is yours, both in law and in fact.

Postscript: What is New?

1. House prices have been standing still or dropping, a reaction to the hectic rises earlier on.

2. It has become difficult to obtain independent advice on endowment insurance, since almost every salesman is tied to one particular company. As you do not expect a Ford car salesman to suggest you buy a Fiat or a bike, do not expect a company representative to advise against his product. Get several quotations and check one against the other, as advised throughout the chapters on money.

Solicitors are not allowed to be tied to one insurance company.

Astonishingly, some intending house buyers do not ask their solicitors for advice before fixing up their mortgage or insurance. This may be false economy.

3. In the near future you may never see a solicitor at all unless you value independent advice. Building societies and banks, which not long ago busily bought firms of estate agents, have recently disposed of a number of their acquisitions; they are now eyeing the possibility of in-house conveyancing – something that a change in the law will almost certainly make possible. Whether they will find this new pursuit profitable remains to be seen. But remember: neither bank nor building society nor finance house is in business to hand out advice for your benefit. The truth of this sad fact is now hitting some of those who took out big mortgages and insurance policies when the rush was on.

You can benefit from their experience. Concentrate on a modest, well-built home, try not to borrow on mortgage more than you can afford, and please make sure that you have read this book before you sign anything.

December 1989

Glossary of Legal Terms

Banker's draft	A cheque issued by a bank, accepted instead of cash on completion of sale.
Completion	The exchange of title deeds against balance of purchase money.
Completion statement	Detailed account of amount payable on completion.
Contract	Agreement between buyer and seller binding both to complete the purchase/sale of the house.
Conveyance	The document which makes the buyer the owner of a house with unregistered title.
Conveyancing	Traditionally, the legal side of buying and selling houses.
Endowment mortgage	Mortgage secured on a house and on an endowment insurance policy.
Ground rent	Annual rent paid for a long lease.
Legal charge	Another word for mortgage.
Mortgage	Legal document pledging house as security for a loan.
Mortgagee	Lender of money on the security of a mortgage. Often a building society, bank or insurance company.
Mortgagor	One who borrows money on mortgage.
Purchaser	The buyer of the house.
Registered land	Land whose title is registered at HM Land Registry and guaranteed by it.
Repayment mortgage	Mortgage loan repaid by instalments.
Restrictive covenants	Don'ts. Restrictions applying to the use of land.
Title deeds	Documents showing ownership of house.
Transfer	The document making the buyer owner of a house with registered title.
Vendor	The seller of the house, usually the owner.

Index